Sauce d'huitres pour un Dindon
Bouilli.

Prenez une Chopine d'huitres, mettez
exprimez leur la Liqueur, que vous
les dans la Besace pour les
conserver
fraîcheur, en suite mettez les
dans l'eau froide, lavez les et
netoyez les bien, mettez les dans
une terrine avec votre Liqueur
dans laquelle vous mettez vous
mettrez un tige de muscade
avec un peu de beurre enveloppé
dans de la farine, et le quart d'un
Citron; faites les bouillir en suite

Benjamin Franklin
Book of Recipes

Hilaire Dubourcq

With line drawings by
Isabel Hutchison

Canopus Publishing Limited
MM

For my wife, Georgina Hunter-Jones,
aviator, writer, and gourmet,
with all my love!

A catalogue record for this book is available from
the British Library.

ISBN 0 9537868 03

Designed and typeset by James Shurmer
in Monotype Baskerville

Printed and bound in Great Britain by the
University Press, Cambridge

Table of Contents

Acknowledgements

I should like to express my sincere gratitude to all those listed below who have contributed to this book in some way or another, in a greater or lesser capacity, with their good suggestions and great help. A very special thank-you goes to Mary, Countess of Bessborough. Without her support this Book of Recipes would not have been so appetizing and elegantly dressed. And as Benjamin Franklin put it: "Eat to please yourself; dress to please others". James Ayres, Richard Bates, Susan Bennett, Brothers-in-Art, Will Brown, Martin Butterworth, Montague Calman, John Campbell-Kease, Ellen R. Cohn, Carolyn Cripps, Raymond Donnell, Diane Durst, Jean-Baptiste Greuze, Jan Henderikse, Rosamund Hitchcock, Paul van der Hoek, Georgina Hunter-Jones, Mr and Mrs Michael Hunter-Jones, Isabel Hutchison, José Kuyper, Robert Landsiedel, Pamela Lassiter Ray, Claude-Anne Lopez, McNulty's Tea and Coffee, Marianne Majerus, Linda Morison, Kate Ohno, Katherine Prior, Marie-Stella Ray, Robin Rees, Sarah Rees, Rex Roberts, Adrian Sassoon, James Shurmer, The Papers of Benjamin Franklin, Thomas Subrink, Rebecca Thurgur, Jeremy Uniacke, United States Department of State, and David Woodrow

Illustrations

The author and publisher wish to thank the following for permission to reproduce illustrations. The front jacket illustration is reproduced courtesy of the United States Department of State (photography by Will Brown) and the National Gallery, London. The illustrations on pages 55 and 60 are from a private collection reproduced courtesy of Adrian Sassoon.

May the 18, 1760

Lord Bessborough's Compliments
to Mr Franklin
and desires the favour of his Company at Dinner
next Sunday

*"No wonder Tom grows fat, th'unwieldy Sinner,
Makes his whole Life but one continual Dinner"*

BENJAMIN FRANKLIN

[4]

Foreword

It was shortly after the Second World War that I first discovered the house in Craven Street, London where Benjamin Franklin lived from 1757 until 1762 and again from 1764 to 1775. Surprisingly, it was the only house still standing in which Franklin had lived, but it was in a run-down state and I resolved to find a way to restore it. Some 40 years later, through the charity I established, the Friends of Benjamin Franklin House, the restoration work began. As I write, the historic day draws near when the house will finally open to the public as a museum and centre of Anglo-American studies.

I love reading about food, so when Hilaire first showed me a draft of this book I was excited by the prospect of learning about the cooking of Benjamin Franklin's day set against a backdrop of 18th-century life. Now the book is finished, I am delighted to see how much he has been able to reveal about Franklin's time in London—what he did, whom he knew, and of course what he ate. But the book spans the whole of Franklin's 84 years, during which time he lived in Boston, Philadelphia and Paris, as well as in London. It covers the main events and great achievements of an extraordinarily rich life, and conveys Franklin's boundless curiosity, his energy, and in particular his love of the pleasures of the table.

As a fellow American, I am aware of the debt we owe to Benjamin Franklin and of his tremendous historical importance. I hope that many visitors will come to the Craven Street house and pay homage to the great scientist, politician, diplomat, and statesman. I also hope that the house will rank alongside such historic jewels as Washington's Mount Vernon, and Jefferson's Monticello and be among those cherished sites associated with the founding fathers of the United States of America.

Hilaire's unique blend of period recipes and Benjamin Franklin's wit and wisdom will delight everyone who, like me, enjoys cooking, but I feel sure it will also take Franklin's life and sayings to a broader audience. It is most fitting that every copy sold should make a contribution to the upkeep and continuing improvement of Benjamin Franklin's House.

Mary, Countess of Bessborough, London, June, 1999

Mary, Countess of Bessborough is the dowager of the 10th Earl of Bessborough who was a direct descendant of William Ponsonby, 2nd Earl of Bessborough. It was the 2nd Earl in his capacity as Joint Postmaster General who in 1765 appointed Benjamin Franklin as Deputy Postmaster and Manager of the Northern District of all His Majesty's Provinces and Dominions on the Continent of North America.

A Note about the Recipes

The *Benjamin Franklin Book of Recipes* has been written with the intention of being anything but a "how to" cookery book. The passages about Franklin's life, provide the background for each chapter's menu, which either features authentic period recipes or ones inspired by 18th-century dishes. Where appropriate, quantities have been given in measures predating the metric system, which was introduced in France in 1791, the year after Franklin's death. The everyday authentic recipes from the 18th century give us an intriguing insight into the dietary pleasures and prejudices of that period. Sidebars add an extra historical dimension to ingredients such as sugar or rice. In the 18th century "a pinch of salt" did not have to be spelled out precisely; it was left to one's own taste and good judgement. If you wanted a hare for a dish, you took a hare, and if a lobster was needed, you chose one at the market of the size you wanted or could find. At that time, therefore, measures were given in vague terms or omitted altogether. Some recipes contain ingredients in large quantities. In the days before refrigeration foods were processed in bulk for preservation. For example when Franklin wrote a recipe for chopped pâté, he proposed "3 pounds of mutton, 50 apples, 2 pounds of currants and one half a pound of the best sugar one can find". When staying in Passy Benjamin Franklin was asked to translate some English recipes into French, such as how to prepare a suckling pig or how to grill cuts of beefsteak. These were recipes of which he was merely the translator and are not accredited to him personally. However, in his *Poor Richard; an Almanack*, which he published over many years until 1758, there are recipes for Dauphiny Soup, rice, Indian corn, all of which have been attributed to Benjamin Franklin. Although taken from other publications, they were judged to be from the publisher's own hand. The same applies to the many witty sayings that appeared in *Poor Richard*. Franklin compiled them but may not necessarily have always written the words himself.

The recipes in this book are either drawn from our historical heritage or inspired by the author's own interpretation of the Life and Liberty of Benjamin Franklin, and his very own Pursuit of Happiness. How many mouths do any of the recipes in this book feed? Well, much depends on how much food you plan to dish up to your guests; always keep in mind, as a rule of thumb, that on average one person will eat about a pound of food per meal. Take it from there and exercise your imagination. However, if you think the kitchen hearth is getting too hot, seek some safer retreat, for this book is fun to read as well as being a source of inspiration to cook fish, fowl and meat.

Chronology

1706   Benjamin Franklin born in Boston, son of Josiah Franklin and Abiah Folger.

1714   Enters Grammar School. Reign of King George I of England, 1714–1727.

1716   Works in his father's tallow-chandlery shop.

1718   Printer's apprentice at his brother James's *New England Courant* in Boston. William Penn dies in England.

1722   Franklin's "Silence Dogood" letters anonymously published in the *New England Courant*.

1723   Leaves Boston and sails to Philadelphia, via New York. Gives up being a vegetarian.

1724   Sails with James Ralph from Philadelphia to London, where he works as a printer for Palmer and later for John Watts.

1725   Visits Don Saltero's Curiosities in Chelsea.

1726   Sails back to Philadelphia, and keeps a journal.

1727   Reign of King George II of England, 1727–1760.

1728   Opens his own printing shop.

1729   Becomes the sole proprietor of the *Pennsylvania Gazette*.

1730   Marries Deborah Read.

1731   Birth of his son William Franklin.

1732   Begins publishing *Poor Richard: An Almanack*. Birth of his son Francis Folger Franklin.

1734   Elected Grand Master of Masons in Pennsylvania.

1736   Death of Francis Folger Franklin from smallpox.

1737   Elected to the Philadelphia Assembly.

1739   Begins work on inventing the Pennsylvania Fireplace.

1742   The Pennsylvania Fireplace made public.

1743 Birth of his daughter Sarah Franklin.

1747 First writes of his electrical experiments with a kite.

1750 Voltaire in Prussia as Frederick the Great's chamberlain.

1751 *Experiments and Observations on Electricity* published in London. Elected to the Pennsylvania Assembly; re-elected until 1764.

1753 Receives the Copley Medal from the Royal Society, and honorary degrees from Harvard and Yale. Appointed Deputy Postmaster General of the Colonies.

1756 Recreates and publishes the recipe for Dauphiny Soup in *Poor Richard: An Almanack*. Elected Fellow of the Royal Society.

1757 Sent to London as agent of the Pennsylvania Assembly to lobby their cause against the Penn proprietors to the Crown. Lodges with Margaret Stevenson and her daughter Mary, also known as Polly, in Craven Street, Strand. William Pitt becomes Prime Minister.

1758 John Baskerville becomes printer to Cambridge University.

1760 Privy Council approves taxation of unsurveyed Penn proprietary estates in Pennsylvania. Reign of King George III of England, 1760–1820.

1761 Pays a visit to the Dutch Republic with his son William. In Leiden, visits Professor Peter van Musschenbroek, the inventor of the Leyden Jar. Invents an improved version of the glass harmonica, Glassy-Chord or Armonica.

1762 Receives an honorary degree from Oxford and returns to Philadelphia.

1763 Tours the northern colonies, inspecting the post offices as Deputy Postmaster General.

1764 Loses his seat in the Assembly. Returns to London as agent for Pennsylvania.

1768 Appointed agent for Georgia.

1769 Named agent for New Jersey. Elected president of the American Philosophical Society.

1770 Becomes agent for Massachusetts. Polly Stevenson marries the physician William Hewson who soon moves into the Craven Street ménage. With William and John Hunter, Hewson founded the American Medical Schools.

1773 Receives the recipe of how to make Parmesan cheese. Boston Tea Party.

1774 Franklin attacked by the Privy Council and dismissed as Deputy Postmaster General. His wife Deborah dies in Philadelphia. Louis XVI becomes King of France.

1775 Franklin returns to Philadelphia. Submits Articles of Confederation of United Colonies. Learns of the battles of Lexington and Concord.

1776 Helps draft and signs the Declaration of Independence. Sets sail for France as American commissioner to negotiate an alliance. Washington crosses the Delaware.

1777 Becomes the darling of Parisian society and French intellectuals and meets Madame Brillon.

1778 Negotiates and signs treaties of alliance and commerce with France. Is introduced to Madame Helvétius. Meets Voltaire in Paris, who gives his grandson Temple his blessing. Antoine Parmentier's potato bread launched.

1779 Formally presents his credentials as Minister Plenipotentiary to the French court. Hosts an Independence Day banquet in Passy. Writes the "Morals of Chess". Captain James Cook dies off the coast of Hawaii.

1780 Recommends honey against obstructions in the veins. Madame Helvétius rejects marriage.

1781 Offers his resignation to Congress, but is turned down. Appointed one of five commissioners to negotiate peace with Britain. The comtesse d'Houdetot invites Franklin to dinner.

1783 Treaty of peace with Britain proclaimed. Margaret Stevenson dies. Witnesses the ascent of the "lighter than air" balloon of the Montgolfier brothers in Paris.

1785 Franklin leaves France for good, and returns to Philadelphia.

1787 Delegate to the Constitutional Convention in Philadelphia.

1789 Outbreak of the French Revolution with the storming of the Bastille.

1790 Benjamin Franklin dies in Philadelphia on 17 April, at the age of 84.

"A full Belly makes a dull Brain:
The Muses starve in a Cook's Shop"
BENJAMIN FRANKLIN

Benjamin Franklin

Benjamin Franklin, one of the founding fathers of the United States of America, was a true product of the Age of Enlightenment. More than that, he was a veritable *homo universalis*. As a young man he saw the world as his oyster and set out to shuck it. Already at a young age he started to devour books of knowledge, even though he had had only two years of formal education (years in which he started in the middle and ended as top of the class). He learned the printing trade at his brother's *New England Courant* and secretly submitted stories to local journals under the pen name of "Silence Dogood". After falling out with his brother over a trivial matter, he ventured down to New York and later to Philadelphia, where he pursued his career in the printing trade. At the age of 17 he sailed to England, where he was again able to find work in a printing house.

Benjamin Franklin was one of those rare men truly interested in all aspects of life. Besides making countless inventions and discoveries, he was forever inquisitive and jovial. In spite of his humble background and often threadbare clothing he was (almost) universally admired. Many years later, when he came back to Philadelphia, he was elected to the Assembly, and as postmaster for the colonies he modernized the US postal service. He formed The Junto, a club for mutual improvement of interested members, and started the *Pennsylvania Gazette* and his *Poor Richard's Almanak* (later in France called *La Science du Bonhomme Richard*). In the almanac he portrayed himself as a didactical man, who preached wisdom, frugality and self-improvement to the public at large. In his later and mellower years he helped Sir Francis Dashwood (later Lord le Despencer) with a revision of the new Prayer Book.

The extraordinary Benjamin Franklin invented a 24-hour clock for navigation, possibly bifocal eyeglasses which he named "double spectacles" and watertight bulkheads for ships. His contribution to music came when he invented the glass armonica. This was an ingenious adaptation of sets of tuned glasses that could be played like a piano, and, although to our ears we may find the sound a little harsh, Gluck, Mozart and Beethoven composed for this new instrument.

Benjamin Franklin invented the Franklin Stove. Installed in the fireplace it allowed the smoke to rise out of the chimney, while radiating heat into the room; hitherto it had been the householder's nose that filled with smoke and much of the heat that travelled up the chimney.

Benjamin Franklin devised many instruments to gauge the temperature of seawater and using these he wrote about the existence of some kind of east-flowing current in the Atlantic. Gradually he plotted maps of this current and gave it the name Gulf Stream.

Having already discovered that lightning was an electrical discharge he sent kites up during thunderstorms and perfected his already famous lightning rod conductor, and thus discovered the positive and negative charge of electricity. This was a gentler use of his much earlier experiments with electricity, which, after the invention in Holland of the Leyden Jar, Franklin had used to kill turkeys with an electrical shock. This electric shock treatment, which made them so unusually tender, was at least a little kinder than the normal 18th-century practice of beating meat to death to make it less tough!

Franklin was awarded honorary degrees by the universities of St Andrews and William and Mary, and an honorary doctorate of civil law by Oxford University.

Benjamin Franklin's love of life and people also contributed to his development into a leading statesman. He was appointed to a committee of five men to draft the Declaration of Independence. Although it is not known if he played any part in its composition, however, it is said that there and then Franklin had stated to his fellow committee members: "We must Hang all Together, or We will Hang Separately".

Dr Franklin signed the Articles of Confederation, the treaty with France, the peace treaty with England, and the Constitution. As America's first ambassador he was sent to France as Minister Plenipotentiary to secure a loan from Louis XVI. In Paris he manifested himself as a diplomat *par excellence* at the Court of Versailles. There, in contrast to his earlier preachings, he lived quite well in Passy, then a suburb of Paris. He had a comfortable remuneration from Congress and this combined with his considerable savings through a life of hard work meant he was then able to live an affluent and sometimes even slightly decadent life, according to his fellow Bostonian, the Puritan John Adams, who visited Benjamin Franklin in Passy rather more for business than for pleasure. Franklin had never bothered to patent his earlier inventions; had he done so he might have been a man of much greater means.

Benjamin Franklin mastered the art of living and was interested in all aspects of life. One can only wonder, notwithstanding his vigorous drive, how a man in his era could have undertaken so many endeavours in a lifetime. Did he really explore so many things? Was he truly the darling of the French Court, where he outwitted the courtesans?

Could all these anecdotes and achievements of Benjamin Franklin be true, even if he were an enlightened *homo universalis*?

Last night I spoke to Benjamin Franklin, and asked him if he had really lived through all these great events:

"Doctor Franklin, is it true what people say and write about you, even 200 years after you deceased?"

"It is irrevocably true, indeed."

"So you appeared at the Court of Versailles without a wig, to present your credentials?"

"I did, what matters is what you have inside your head, not on top of it."

"Doctor Franklin, having advocated frugality all your life, how do you reconcile that with the way you later lived like a god in France?"

"Frugality is a virtue I never could acquire myself."

Whimsical Will once fancy'd he was ill,

The Doctor's call'd, who thus examin'd Will;

How is your Appetite? O, as to that

I eat right heartily, you see I'm fat.

How is your Sleep anights? 'Tis sound and good;

I eat, drink, sleep as well as e'er I cou'd.

Well, says the Doctor, clapping on his Hat;

I'll give you something shall remove all that.

Poor Richard's Almanak, 1736

The Little House off the Strand

When Benjamin Franklin returned to London in 1757 after an absence of more than three decades, he settled in a small terraced house, built in 1730 on the former estate of the earls of Craven. His landlady at Craven Street was Margaret Stevenson, a widow, who had signed the lease to the house in 1748, and lived there with her daughter Mary, also known as Polly. Craven Street, formerly Spur Alley, lies just off the Strand on the west side of Charing Cross Station and around the corner from Trafalgar Square. In Franklin's day the square and station were not yet a part of London's city plan. Craven Street ran then between the Strand and the river with Hungerford Market to the east, where carts were carrying meat and produce from the wharf to market. The old Globe tavern, a favourite meeting place in those days, appears to have stood at the corner of Craven Street and the Strand. Craven Street was ideal for Franklin, being within walking distance of Whitehall and the Houses of Parliament.

In the coffee houses nearby, in Fleet Street and the Strand, he was well known and loved for his wisdom, kindness and wit. That was true also of the Pennsylvania Coffee House on Birchin Lane, where he received much of the mail from his American correspondents. In Craven Street he enjoyed intellectually stimulating visits from many distinguished members of The Royal Society and fought tirelessly on behalf of Pennsylvania and later of other American colonies.

In 1775 Benjamin Franklin sailed back to Philadelphia. He had failed in what had been one of his prime objectives; to keep the Colonies united within the British Empire.

Much later in his long life, during his time in Passy, then on the outskirts of Paris, Benjamin Franklin wrote in 1779 to Margaret Stevenson, with whom he had spent so much time under the same roof in Craven Street:

It is always with great Pleasure when I think of our long continu'd Friendship, which had not the least Interruption in the Course of Twenty Years (some of the happiest of my Life) that I spent under your Roof and in your Company. If I do not write to you as often as I us'd to do when I happen'd to be absent from you, it is owing partly to the present Difficulty of sure Communication, & partly to an Apprehension of some possible Inconvenience that my Correspondence might occasion you. Be assured, my dear Friend, that my Regard, Esteem, & Affection for you are not in the least impair'd or diminish'd, and that if Circumstances

[13]

would permit, nothing wuld afford me so much Satisfaction, as to be with you in the same House, & to experience again your faithful tender Care & Attention to my Interests, Health & Comfortable Living, which so long & steadily attach'd me to you, & which I shall ever remember with Gratitude.

I thought I had mention'd to you before; (and I believe I did, tho' my Letter may have miscarried) that I had received the white Cloth Suit, the Sword, & the Saddle for Temple, all in good Order. I mention them now again because Polly tells me you had not heard of their Arrival. And I repeat my Thanks for your Care in sending them. I wore the Clothes a good deal last Summer. —There is one more that I wish to have, if you should meet with an Opportunity of sending it. I mean the Copper Pot lin'd with Silver to roast Fowls in by means of a Heater. I should also be glad of the Piece of Elephant's Tooth. It is old Ivory, perhaps of

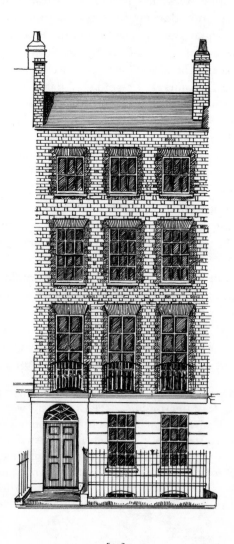

the Time before the Flood, & would be a Rarity to some Friends here: But I doubt you will not be able to send them.

I rejoice to learn that your Health is establish'd, & that you live pleasantly in a Country Town with agreable Neighbours, & have your Dear Children about you. My Love to every one of them. I long to see them and you; but the Times do not permit me the Hope of it. —Why do you never write to me? I us'd to love to read your Letters, regret your long Silence. They were season'd with good Sense and Friendship, & even your Spelling pleas's me: Polly knows I think the worst Spelling is the best.

Since my coming here, I have been told, that Mr Henley the Linen Draper had said, on my going to America, that I had gone away in his Debt. I can hardly believe it. Let me know if you have heard of such a Thing, & what is the meaning of it. I thought he had been fully paid, & I still think so, & shall till I am assur'd of the contrary. —Let me know at the same time how my Account stands with you.

You wish to know how I live. It is in a fine House, situated in a neat Village, on high Ground, half a Mile from Paris, with a large Garden to walk in. I have abundance of Acquaintance, dine abroad Six Days in seven. Sundays I reserve to dine at home, with such Americans as pass this Way; & I then have my Grandson Ben, with some other American Children from his School: If being treated with all the Politeness of France, & the apparent Respect & Esteem of all Ranks, from the highest to the lowest, can make a Man happy, I ought to be so. Indeed I have nothing to complain but of a little too much Business, & the Want of that Order and Oeconomy in my Family, that reign'd in it when under your prudent Direction. My Paper gives me only Room to add, that I am ever Yours most affectionately.

Benjamin Franklin, the man who had written *The Art of Making Money Plenty in Every Man's Pocket* and a shorter version called *The Way to Wealth*, translated into at least fifteen other languages, owned a considerable amount of real estate by the time of his death. Lands in Nova Scotia, Pennsylvania and Georgia, several houses in Philadelphia and one in Boston. However, it is the house at 36 Craven Street in London (which he did not own), that is the sole surviving house of those in which he had lived. Franklin's birthplace on Milk Street in Boston burned down in 1810. His house and printing office in Philadelphia, which he built with the help of his wife Deborah, are also no longer with us, nor is the Hotel de Valentinois in Passy where he resided as America's Minister Plenipotentiary to France. Passy was in those days a suburban village, an idyllic place "about half an hour's Drive from the City", with a view over the Seine in the midst of the countryside. Today Passy is solidly incorporated as a part of the 16th *arrondissement* of Paris. In 1913, the London Council Housing Division discovered, much to their embarrassment, that they had Franklin's red wall plaque on the wrong house in Craven Street. The correct house, identified from his landlady's historic lease, which she signed in 1748, was two up from Craven Lane (now Craven Passage) and the plaque was removed from No. 7 to No. 36. In 18th-century London numbers were not used on houses.

The Georgian house on Craven Street, which was remodelled during the Regency period and in which Franklin spent "some of the happiest years of his life", is at last being preserved as a museum; an architectural memorial to the Life & Liberty and the Pursuit of Happiness of one of America's founding fathers: Benjamin Franklin.

In Craven Street, Strand, ten attorneys find place,
And ten dark coal barges are moor'd at its base;
Fly, Honesty, fly! seek some safer retreat,
For there's craft in the river and craft in the street.

James Smith (author and humorist) in 1839.

Alfreton 15th Jan 1772

Dear Sir,

I hope this will find you well in Craven Street, after a Summer of rambling, in which I have been so unfortunate as not to see you; in your first ramble thro' Derbyshire I was in Scotland; in your last, at home, and sick of not seeing you.

I am my Self very well, my Wife yet poorly; wishes to hear that Mrs Stevenson holds stout; and yesterday sent a Turkey by Clarks Wagon to the Ax in Aldermanbury; to regale you. Our best joint Complements with those of this season attend your self and Mrs Stevenson and I am Dear Sir Yours Sincerely and affectionately.

Anth Tissington

Boston Party

MILK STREET FISH AND CLAM CHOWDER

~

CHOPPED PÂTÉ

~

BOSTON SCROD CAKES

~

MAPLE FRUIT SALAD

Boston was only seventy-five years old when Benjamin Franklin was born there in 1706 and its inhabitants in those days lived in relative peace. Franklin grew up in a poor household, where his father Josiah was a "Tallow Chandler and Sope-Boiler". The Franklin family lived in a tiny house on Milk Street, where Josiah taught his young son the virtues of Puritan life; worldly goods had to be obtained in an honest way, kept safely and money spent thriftily. Boston's streets were narrow; there were open sewers, occasional epidemics, and a high birth mortality rate. During the cold winters when the harbour was frozen over, the houses were poorly heated owing to the scarcity of firewood. Despite these hardships, life to the Boston Puritans seemed a lot better than that in London. In those days, when home-made cider was drunk by the poor, rum by the better off and imported wine by the rich, the sixteen-year-old Benjamin came across a book written by a certain Tryon, recommending a vegetable diet.

I determined to go into it. My Brother being yet unmarried, did not keep House, but boarded himself and his Apprentices in another Family. My refusing to eat Flesh occasioned an Inconveniency, and I was frequently chid for my singularity. I made my self acquainted with Tryon's Manner of preparing some of his Dishes, such as Boiling Potatoes or Rice, making Hasty Pudding, and a few others, and then propos'd to my Brother, that if he would give me Weekly half the Money he paid for my Board I would board my self. He instantly agreed to it, and I presently found that I could save half what he paid me. This was an additional Fund for buying Books: But I had another Advantage in it. My Brother and the rest going from the Printing House to their Meals, I remain'd there alone, and dispatching presently my light Repast, (which often was no more than a Brisket or a Slice of Bread, a Handful of Raisins or a Tart from the Pastry Cook's, and a Glass of Water) had the rest of the Time till their Return, for Study, in which I made the greater Progress from that greater Clearness of Head and quicker Apprehension which usually attend Temperance in Eating and drinking.

A year later at the age of seventeen, Benjamin Franklin left Boston and ran away to Philadelphia. It was during this voyage, off Block Island, when his "rational thinking" persuaded him to consider his refusal to eat "animal food" as something of the past. On the final leg of his journey he stopped near Burlington where an old woman asked him into her house and offered him dinner. There Benjamin dined gratefully on ox cheek.

Milk Street Fish and Clam Chowder

The word chowder may come from the French word *chaudière*, which in olden days was a big copper or iron cauldron used for all-purpose cooking and either hung from a hook above the fireplace or was placed in the smouldering ashes on the hearth.

The stock

2 lbs fish heads, bones and trimmings of cod, haddock,
or any non-oily white fish ~ 1 carrot, sliced ~ 1 onion, sliced
1 stick of celery, sliced ~ ½ cup of clam juice
½ cup of dry white wine ~ 2 bay leaves
1 teaspoonwhite peppercorns ~ 1 teaspoon coarse salt

Rinse the pieces of fish and remove the gills from the fish heads. Place all pieces of fish in a large saucepan with the vegetables, bay leaves, peppercorns and salt. Pour in the clam juice and wine, and add 4 pints of water to it. Bring gently to the boil. After 3 to 4 minutes of boiling, scrape off the pieces of fish from the bones and set aside. Bring the saucepan back to a boil and simmer for 30 minutes while scooping off the scum as it rises to the surface. Strain. Discard the bones, vegetables, bay leaves and peppercorns. This recipe gives you about a quart of fish stock.

The chowder

½ lb cod fillets ~ ½ lb haddock fillets
1 cup minced Little Neck clams ~ 1 cup chopped bacon
1 cup chopped onion ~ 2½ cups diced raw potatoes ~ 1 tablespoon butter
1 teaspoon salt ~ 1 teaspoon pepper ~ 1 cup milk ~ 1 cup heavy cream
¼ cup chopped parsley ~ 1 cup fish stock

Remove skin and bones from the fillets. Cut into 1-inch cube pieces. Fry bacon in a saucepan until crisp and add onions until they are tender and golden brown.

Add potatoes and water, fish stock, salt, pepper. Simmer until the potatoes are tender. Add the fish pieces and minced clams and simmer until cooked. Add milk, heavy cream, butter and simmer softly for 10–15 minutes. Serve and garnish with chopped parsley.

Chopped Pâté

3 lbs mutton, finely chopped
2 lbs currants, well washed and dried near the oven
50 apples, cored, peeled, and finely chopped
½ lb sugar, the best, and finely grated ~ ¼ oz nutmeg
¼ oz cloves, all of this finely chopped

"Combine all in a big pot, stir, add half a glass of brandy and half a glass of Malaga wine. Transfer all of this to a ceramic container. Cover your platter with a layer of dough, cover that with a layer (not too thick) of the mixture, then a layer of thinly sliced lemon, another layer of the chopped mixture and one of thinly sliced orange peel. On top of this a light layer of the mixture, and the juice of an orange or a lemon. One more layer of dough and put the whole thing in the oven."

Boston Scrod Cakes

2 cups cooked and flaked scrod (or flounder)
1 tablespoon diced scallions ~ 1 tablespoon finely diced celery
2 beaten eggs ~ 1 tablespoon Worcestershire sauce
1 teaspoon Tabasco ~ ½ tablespoon Dijon mustard ~ ⅓ cup flour
2 teaspoons pepper ~ 1 teaspoon salt

Mix the scrod (flounder), scallions, and celery in a glass bowl. Add the beaten eggs, Dijon mustard, Worcestershire sauce, and Tabasco. Mix well and shape the mixture into small cakes. Coat the cakes lightly with flour and fry in hot butter until golden brown.

Maple Fruit Salad

It was not until during the eighteenth century that raw fruit was considered by physicians safe and healthy to eat. Once it was thought to be the cause of colic and even to spread the plague.

2 grapefruit ~ 3 oranges ~ 1 lime (juice and zest)
1 lemon (juice and zest) ~ 1 head of Boston lettuce
3 tablespoons maple syrup ~ 3 tablespoons walnut oil
1 teaspoon Dijon mustard ~ pepper and salt ~ 1 cup chopped walnuts

Rinse the lettuce leaves and break into large pieces. Peel, slice and quarter the grapefruits and oranges. Arrange the citrus pieces on the bed of lettuce.

For the dressing, mix walnut oil, juices of lemon and lime, Dijon mustard, pepper and salt to taste. Pour over the fruit and lettuce. Sprinkle chopped pieces of walnut as topping over the salad and add grated pieces of the lemon and lime zest. To finish off, swirl streaks of maple syrup over toppings and salad.

"Fruit is essential for maintaining gums and skin"

BENJAMIN FRANKLIN

[BOURBON]

The most famous American whiskey is bourbon. It is America's native spirit and goes back to the pioneer days when early Irish and Scottish settlers brought their whiskey distilling traditions to western Pennsylvania. Whiskey was being produced throughout the colonies, but it was west of the Alleghenies where bourbon's history began with the 1794 Whiskey Rebellion. Alexander Hamilton had imposed an excise tax on whiskey in 1791, which had caused an uprising by settlers. George Washington, a whiskey producer himself at the time, was forced to send in the Continental Army to crush the rebellion. The settlers were put down easily, many arrests were made, and two rebels were convicted of treason, but President Washington later pardoned them. To save face Washington later gave the settlers incentives to move down to Kentucky (then a part of Virginia), where Governor Thomas Jefferson offered the pioneers 60 acres of land to grow corn in Bourbon County. Early whiskey was primarily made from rye, but a corn crop from 60 acres turned out to be too much for consumption and too perishable to transport to distant markets. Therefore, the surplus corn was turned into whiskey, and so it was in Bourbon County, Kentucky, named after the French royal family, that bourbon whiskey was born.

❦ ❦ ❦

THE PENNSYLVANIA GAZETTE, January 4 to December 27, 1739

Advertisement

Benjamin Franklin, Printer, is removed from the House he lately dwelt in, four Doors nearer the River, on the same side of the Street.

Receipt for the Ague or Intermitting Fever
By Benjamin Franklin

Take on Ounce of good Peruvian Bark, finely levigated; make it into an Electuary with Treacle or Molasses, mixing therewith twenty or thirty Drops of Laudanum, take this at about six or eight Doses two or three Hours apart, washing it down with a Glass of Madeira or red Wine. If any thing like Jaundice, or Yellowness about the Eyes remains, chew Rhubarb a few Mornings.

A Printer's Breakfast

WATER-GRUEL

~

JUSTIFIED EGGS WITH TOAST

~

BENJAMIN FRANKLIN'S SECRET COFFEE BLEND

Benjamin Franklin sailed from Philadelphia to London in 1724, sent by the Philadelphia printer Keimer to buy printing equipment. When he arrived, he discovered Keimer's letters of credit had not been left in the captain's trunk. So the young Benjamin was forced to find employment, at first at Palmer's, a then famous printing house in Bartholomew Close. Samuel Palmer was very impressed with him. Later he went to work for another printer called Watts. Here the young Franklin had his first clashes with his fellow printers.

> At my first Admission into this Printing House, I took to working at Press, imagining I felt a Want of the Bodily Exercise I had been us'd to in America, where Presswork is mix'd with Composing. I drank only Water; the other Workmen, near 50 in Number, were great Guzzlers of Beer. On occasion I carried up and down Stairs a large Form of Types in each Hand, when others carried but one in both Hands. They wonder'd to see from this and several Instances that the Water-American, as they call'd me was stronger than themselves who drank strong Beer.

We had an Alehouse Boy who attended always in the House to supply the Workmen. My Companion at the Press, drank every day a Pint before Breakfast, a Pint at Breakfast with his Bread and Cheese; a Pint between Breakfast and Dinner; a Pint at Dinner; a Pint in the Afternoon about Six o'Clock, and another when he had done his Day's-Work. I thought it a detestable Custom. But it was necessary, he suppos'd, to drink strong Beer that he might be strong to Labour. I endeavour'd to convince him that the Bodily Strength afforded by Beer could only be in Proportion to the Grain or Flour of the Barley dissolved in the Water of which it was made. Flour is a Penny-worth of Bread, and therefore if he would eat that with a Pint of Water, it would give him more Strength than a Quart of Beer. He drank on however, and had 4 or 5 Shillings to pay out of his Wages every Saturday Night for that muddling Liquor; an Expense I was free from. And thus these poor Devils keep themselves always under.

Watts after some Weeks desiring to have me in the Composing Room, I left the Pressmen. A new Bienvenue or Sum for Drink, being 5s., was demanded from me by the Compositors. I thought it an Imposition, as I had paid below. The Master thought it too, and forbad my Paying it. I stood out two or three Weeks, was accordingly considered as an Excommunicate, and had so many little Pieces of private Mischief done to me, by mixing my Sorts, transposing my Pages, breaking my Matter, &c, &c. if I were ever so little out of the Room, and all ascrib'd to the Chapel Ghost, which they said ever haunted those not regularly admitted, that notwithstanding the Master's Protection, I found myself oblig'd to comply and pay the Money; convinc'd of the Folly of being on ill Terms with those one is to live with continually. I was now on a fair Footing with them, and soon acquir'd considerable Influence. I propos'd some reasonable Alterations in their Chapel Laws, and carried them against all Opposition. From my Example a great Part of them, left their muddling Breakfast of Beer and Bread and Cheese, finding they could with me be supply'd from a neighbouring House with a large Porringer of hot Water-gruel, sprinkled with Pepper, crumb'd with Bread, and a Bit of Butter in it, for half the Price of a Pint of Beer, viz three halfpence. This was a more comfortable as well as cheaper Breakfast, and kept their Heads clearer.

Water-Gruel

"You must take a Pint of Water, and a large Spoonful of Oatmeal; then stir it together, and let it boil up three or four Times, stirring it often. Don't let it boil over, then strain it through a Sieve. Salt it to your Palate, put in a good Piece of Fresh Butter, brue it with a Spoon till the Butter is all melted. Then it will be fine and smooth, and very good. Some love a little Pepper in it."

"Rather go to bed supperless, than run in debt for a Breakfast"
BENJAMIN FRANKLIN

Justified Eggs with Toast

2 eggs ~ 2 tablespoons of butter ~ 1 cup soured cream
½ teaspoon corn starch ~ ⅓ cup shredded cheddar cheese
1 teaspoon of salt ~ 1 teaspoon of pepper ~ 2 teaspoon of chopped chives
2 teaspoon of chopped parsley ~ 4 slices sour bread toast

Take two small ramekins and rub the inside with butter. Melt slowly *au bain-marie* and carefully drop an egg into each. Cook as slowly as possible. Put the soured cream into a saucepan and heat until it reduces. Mix the corn starch with a little water and stir into the soured cream. Keep cooking until it starts to thicken. Stir in the parsley and chives, and add salt and pepper. When the eggs are set, pour in the sauce and serve with the sour bread toast.

"An Egg today is better than a Hen tomorrow"   BENJAMIN FRANKLIN

Benjamin Franklin's Secret Coffee Blend

½ lb Ethiopian Yirgacheffe ~ ¼ lb Jamacan High Mountain
¼ lb Santo Domingo

In the 18th century coffee and tea were referred to as "Slip Slop" and were quite fashionable drinks and more expensive than ale or gin. During his Craven Street days Benjamin Franklin patronized many a coffee house on the Strand and in Fleet Street. Coffee houses were places where people gathered together and discussed the topics of the day. These meeting places were always hotbeds of political, economical and literary debate. This created a demand for shipping news from overseas and for foreign and domestic news items. It was therefore in the coffee houses that the first daily newspapers started to appear. In 1724 London had three daily papers and by 1776 there were a total of 53 newspapers in London alone. In the 18th-century journal the *London Spy* an eye witness account appeared:

'Come with me' said my friend, 'and I will show you my favourite coffee house. Since you are a stranger in the town it will amuse you' … as if it was speaking, he reached the door of the coffee house in question. The entry was dark, so that we were hard put to it not to stumble. Mounting a few steps, we made our way into a big room which was equipped in an old-fashioned way. There was a rabble going hither and thither, reminding me of a swarm of rats in a ruinous cheese-store. Some came, others went; some were scribbling, others were talking; some were drinking (coffee), some smoking, and some arguing; the whole place stank of tobacco like the cabin of a barge. On the corner of a long table, close by the armchair, was lying a Bible … Besides it were earthenware pitchers, long clay pipes, a little fire on the hearth, and over it the huge coffee-pot. Beneath a small book-shelf, on which were bottles, cups, and an advertisement for a beautifier to improve the complexion, was hanging a parliamentary ordinance against drinking and the use of bad language. The walls were decorated with gilt frames, much as a smithy is decorated with horseshoes. In the frames were rarities; phials of yellow elixir, favourite pills and hair-tonics, packets of snuff, tooth-powder made of coffee-grounds, caramels and cough lozenges. Had not my friend told me that he brought me to a coffeehouse, I would have regarded the place as a big booth of cheap-jack.… When I had sat there for a while, and taken in my surroundings, I myself felt inclined for a cup of coffee.

Benjamin Franklin had the following to say about coffee in a letter from London to John Ellis in 1774:

In this same Year (1652) one of Mr. Edwards, a Turky Merchant, brought home with him a Greek Servant, who understood the roasting and making of Coffee, till then unknown in England. This servant was the first who sold Coffee, and kept a House for that purpose in London. The first Mention of Coffee in our Statute Books is Anno 1660. In 1675 King Charles issued a Proclamation to shut up the Coffeehouses, but in a few Days suspended that Proclamation by a second. They were charg'd with being Seminaries of Sedition. In 1718 the Dutch Colony at Surinam began first to plant Coffee. In 1732 it was cultivated in Jamaica, and an Act passed to encourage its Growth there. It had been cultivated before by the French at Martinica, Hispaniola and Ile Bourbon.

Dr Franklin presents his Compliments to Mr Ellis, and sends him all the Information he has concerning Coffee. It is collected from Anderson's History of Commerce. And he knows of no other Book that gives any Account of it.

"Pride breakfasted with Plenty, dined with Poverty, supped with Infamy"   BENJAMIN FRANKLIN

Versailles, May 1, 1778

Monsieur Le docteur

Enclosed are some nabob or fine rice and a hundred beans from the Cape of Good Hope, the best legume of their kind. …

… Experience has taught me. In my times in the Indies I used to breakfast with my white men on a bowl of strong coffee with rice, sugar, a bottle or two of brandy depending on the number of people, and when possible one or two dozen egg yolks well beaten. With this start I could roam the woods all day in search of runaway slaves, and nobody was hungry or thirsty.

I have the honor of being with respect Monsieur le docteur Your very humble and very obedient servant.

De Reine, Ancien Capt.

[COFFEE]

The coffee plant was known before 1000 AD in Abyssinia by members of the Galla tribe, where its fruit was used in food and wine. The legend has it that coffee was first discovered in the mountains of Yemen by a herd of goats belonging to a monastery. The goats had returned from the mountains to the monastery and instead of falling asleep, they danced and leaped around through the night. Up in the mountains they had been eating from a shrub from which the flowers had died and small berries had appeared. Inside each berry there was a small kernel, the coffee bean. Coffee is grown at high altitudes with abundant rainfall, warm temperatures, rich soil and adequate shading. The coffee is harvested by hand at the peak of its ripeness, sorted to remove undesirable beans, and be cleaned. The beans are then graded and separated by size and density; only the highest grades are chosen for specialty use. The roasting of the coffee beans takes place in a controlled environment to bring out an even colour and the best flavour; little or no water is used during the roasting.

Around 1000 AD the first coffee plantations were set up in Arabia and for the first time the beans were boiled, creating a drink called "quahwa". Later the Ottoman Turks introduced coffee to Constantinople and in 1475 the world's first coffee house "Kiva Han" was opened there. Coffee first became known to the Europeans during the Crusades. The first European coffee house opened in Vienna in 1529, after the retreating Turkish army left a bag of coffee beans behind. Here, for the first time, the coffee grounds were filtered and sweetening and milk were added to the beverage. A hundred years later coffee was brought to Italy by traders and was believed by some Christians to be the devil's libation. The pope decided to taste the coffee, before banishing it, but liked it so much, he decided to baptise it. Hence making coffee an acceptable beverage for Christians. In 1652 the first coffee house opened in London when the merchant Mr Edwards set up his Greek servant, Pasqua Rosee, as the first coffee-man in St Michael's Alley off Cornhill. People gravitated towards it to join in drinking the "Black Apollo". In New York coffee had replaced ale as the favourite beverage for breakfast. London boasted nearly 2,000 coffee establishments a hundred years later. That is when King Charles II decided to ban coffee houses, as being revolutionary hotbeds. The ban only lasted 11 days.

In the early 18th century, Dutch traders provided the French with a coffee bush, and the French later set up plantations on the West Indian island of Martinique. At the same time, in Germany women were being prevented from drinking coffee, which was believed to make them infertile. Johann Sebastian Bach's response was his composition of his "Kaffee-Kantate", with the aria:

"Ah, how sweet coffee tastes. Lovelier than a thousand kisses, far sweeter than muscatel wine! I must have my coffee!"

THE PENNSYLVANIA GAZETTE, July 31. 1735

Advertisement

Very Good COFFEE sold by the Printer hereof.

THE RULES AND ORDERS OF THE COFFEE HOUSE

Enter sirs freely, But first if you please,
Pursue our Civil-Orders which are these:
First, gentry, tradesmen, all are welcome hither,
And may without affront sit down together;
Pre-eminence of place, none here should mind,
But take the next fit seat that he can find;
Nor need any, if Finer Persons come,
Rise up to assigne to them his room;
To limit men's Expence we think not fair,
But let him forfeit twelve-pence that shall swear;
He that shall any Quarrel here begin,
Shall give each man a dish t'atone the sin;
And so shall he, whose complements extend
So far to drink in COFFEE to his Friend;
Let noise of loud disputes be quite forborn,
No Maudlin Lovers here in Corners mourn,
But all be brisk, and talk, but not too much.
On Sacred Things, let none presume to touch,
Nor profane Scriptures, nor saucily wrong
Affairs of State with an irreverent tongue:
Let mirth be innocent, and each man see
That all his jests without reflection be;
To keep the House more quiet and from blame,
We banish hence Cards, Dice and every Game:
Nor can allow of Wage(r)s that exceed
Five Shillings, which oft-time much trouble breed;
Let all that's lost, or forfeited, be spent
In such Good Liquor as the House doth vent,
And Customers endeavour to their powers,
For to observe still seasonable hours.
Lastly, let each man what he calls for Pay,
And so you're welcome to come every day.

Double Specs

TWO ĐRESS'D PLOVERS (OR GUINEA FOWL)

~

JUGGED HARE

~

SWEET POTATO PIE

~

FRANKLIN'S HOT FLANNEL

When Benjamin Franklin had grown old and had to wear his spectacles to read, he noticed that objects any distance away were blurred. He could not bring the face of his clock on the other side of the room into focus. To his amazement he also noticed that without his lenses he could see the clock face clearly, even through plain glass. So he constructed a pair of glasses with a piece of plain glass in the upper parts and in the lower section a lens for reading. Using these he could read and look away in clarity without having to remove his glasses. He called his new invention "double spectacles", which, a hundred years after his death, came to be known as bifocals.

This story has been the popular belief, but it is not clear whether Franklin was the sole inventor. During his sojoun at Passy he wrote to his dear friend and philanthropist George Whately:

"... I cannot distinguish a Letter even of a Large Print; but I am happy in the Invention of Double Spectacles, which serving for distant objects as well as near ones, make my Eyes as useful to me as ever were: If all other Defects and Infirmities were as easily and cheaply remedied, it would be worth while for Friends to live a good deal longer ..."

Here Franklin spoke of himself being "happy in the Invention" rather than being the inventor. It is also known that quite a few of Franklin's acquaintances wore bifocals. London instrument maker Peter Dollond constructed them for Sir Joshua Reynolds the first President of the Royal Academy. Samuel Pierce had made them for Benjamin West, the second President of the Royal Academy and commented that West was in the habit of using "divided glasses". Peter Dollond, however, was of the opinion that double specs "can only serve particular Eyes not in general", which George Whately relayed to Franklin:

"... By M. Dollond's Saying, that my double Spectacles can only serve particular Eyes, I doubt he has not been rightly informed of their Construction. I imagine it will be found pretty generally true, that the same Convexity of Glass, through which Man sees clearest and best at the distance proper for reading, is not best for greater distances. I therefore had formerly two Pair of Spectacles, which I shifted occasionally, as in travelling I sometimes read, and often wanted to regard the Prospects. Finding the Change troublesome, and not always sufficiently ready, I had the Glasses cut and half of each kind associated in the same circle. By this Means, as I wear my Spectacles constantly, I have only to move my Eyes up or down as I want to see distinctly far or near, the proper Glasses being always ready. This I find more particularly convenient since my being in France, the Glasses that serve me best at Table to see what I eat, not being the best to see the Faces of those on the other Side of the Table who speak to me; and when ones Ears are not well accustom'd to the Sounds of a Language, a Sight of the Movements in the Features of him that speaks helps to explain; so that I understand French better by the Help of my Spectacles."

Franklin left us a characteristic account of his habitual use of his spectacles:

"Figure me in your mind as jolly as formerley, and as strong and hearty, only a few Years older; being very plainly dress'd, wearing my thin gray strait Hair, that peeps out from under my only Coiffure, a fine Fur Cap, which comes down to my Forehead and almost to my Spectacles ..."

Two Dress'd Plovers (or Guinea Fowl)

"To two Plovers [or guinea fowl] take two Artichoke-Bottoms boiled, some Chestnuts roasted and blanched, some Skirrets [or use parsnip] boiled, cut all very small. Mix it with some Marrow or Beef Sewet, and the Yolks of two hard Eggs. Chop all together, season with Pepper, Salt, Nutmeg and a little Sweet Herbs. Fill the Bodies of the Plovers [or guinea fowl], lay them in a Sauce-pan, and put to them a Pint of Gravy, a Glass of White Wine, a Blade or two of Mace, some roasted Chestnuts blanched, and Artichoke-Bottoms cut into Quarters, two or three Yolks of hard Eggs, and a little Juice of Lemon. Cover them close, and let them stew very softly for an Hour. If you find the Sauce is not thick enough, take a Piece of Butter rolled in Flour, and put it into the Sauce, shake it round, and when it is thick take up your Plovers [or guinea fowl] and pour the Sauce over them. Garnish with roasted Chestnuts. Or you may roast your Plovers [or guinea fowl] as you do any other Fowl."

Jugged Hare

1 hare ~ 1 onion stuck with cloves ~ 4 oz bacon
3 cloves of crushed garlic ~ 4 blades of mace ~ 4 tablespoons of cognac
1 cup of port ~ 1 pint of stock ~ 3 tablespoons butter
3 tablespoons soured cream ~ 2 tablespoons red currant jelly
2 teaspoons white pepper ~ 2 teaspoons salt

The marinade:
1½ pints of red wine ~ 2 bundles of sweet herbs
2 chopped shallots ~ 1 bay leaf ~ 4 tablespoons olive oil

Cut the hare into little pieces and save the blood. Marinate the meat in the red wine with the olive oil, a bundle of sweet herbs, chopped shallot and the bay leaf, overnight. Cut the bacon into fine strips and fry in butter with the crushed garlic. Take the pieces of marinated hare and dry them thoroughly with a towel. Remove the bacon and garlic from the frying pan and drain on a towel. Brown the pieces of hare quickly in the same frying pan in the butter with the bacon drippings. Take an ovenproof earthenware jug and pack in the fried pieces of hare, with the clove studded onion, the fried bacon and garlic, the blades of mace, a bundle of sweet herbs, the cognac, and pepper and salt. Pour in enough stock to cover the meat. Close the jug tightly and cook in a 350°F (gas mark 4) oven for 3 hours. When cooked, pour out the juices from the jug into a saucepan, and take out the blades of mace, the onion and the small bundle of sweet herbs. Reduce the juices and add soured cream, the port and the hare's blood to it. Reduce some more and finally add the red currant jelly to give the sauce a smooth

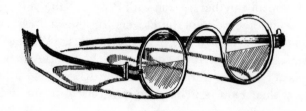

consistency. Arrange the pieces of hare in a shallow casserole and pour over the sauce. Serve with sautéed sliced mushrooms in the sauce around the pieces and sprinkle the dish with fresh chopped parsley.

"Beware of Meat twice boil'd, and an old Foe reconcil'd"
BENJAMIN FRANKLIN

Sweet Potato Pie

2 cups cooked sweet potatoes ~ 1 cup sugar ~ 2 tablespoons molasses
½ teaspoon salt ~ 2 teaspoons ground cinnamon
1 teaspoon ground nutmeg ~ ½ teaspoon ground cloves

Mash the cooked potatoes and combine with the heavy cream, the beaten eggs, sugar and molasses. Stir in the salt and spices and spread the mixture evenly out in an unbaked piecrust. Bake in a pre-heated 450°F oven (gas mark 8) for 10 minutes and reduce to 350°F (gas mark 4) and continue to bake for 30 minutes, or until an inserted knife point comes out clean.

"Men take more pains to mask than mend"   BENJAMIN FRANKLIN

Franklin's Hot Flannel

1 Large Jigger of Gin ~ 1 Pint of warmed Ale ~ 3 oz of Sugar
1 Pinch of Nutmeg

Add gin to pint of warmed ale. Stir in sugar and nutmeg. Serve.

"Eat not to dullness; drink not to elevation"   BENJAMIN FRANKLIN

[PORT]

The first vines introduced into Portugal were the Pinot Noir, by Count Henry of Burgundy. The rich red wine was most likely the forerunner of the ports. Today's ports are a blend of red wine and brandy. The first shipment of the wine to England was in 1353, when a treaty was signed, allowing Portuguese fishermen to fish for cod off the English coast in return for the importation of wine. This trade alliance was sealed in 1373, when a Treaty of Perpetual Friendship was formed and signed by the two countries. By the end of the 16th century, England controlled much of the wine growing trade in Portugal and had founded its first association in Oporto, dealing in wine, cotton, wheat and salted fish.

The first entry in the Oporto Customs House of port shipped to England was in 1678, by two sons of a Liverpool wine merchant. They visited the monastery in Lamego, where the abbot served them "Priest Port", hitherto unknown to the English. The two men bought up all the wine and shipped it to England, after adding a little brandy to it. In 1703 the Methuen Treaty between Portugal and England was signed, which was to be of great commercial significance. It allowed English woollen cloth to be imported to Portugal duty free, in return for which Portuguese wines entered England for a third less duty than the French wines. It was therefore much to this treaty that port owed its great popularity in 18th-century England.

[GIN]

The origins of gin can be traced to 17th-century Holland, where unaged grain alcohol mixed with the oils of the juniper berry was known as genever, and still is. English soldiers brought this drink back to England and introduced it as an inexpensive, pleasant tasting spirit, which eventually became the national drink known as gin. Gin became popular in the British colonies, where, mixed with quinine containing tonic water, it would soften the effects of malaria.

Dry gin, which London distillers developed in 1831, and quite different from Dutch genever, was made by a process of continuous distillation. This new method gave gin a purer, unsweetened or drier taste. Until then sugars had been used to counteract the rougher flavours of old distillation methods. Hence London Dry Gin came into being, Today, however, the term has become generic describing a style rather than a location.

❦ ❦ ❦

THE PENNSYLVANIA GAZETTE, 1742

Advertisement

Just Imported, And to be Sold by John Breintnal, in Chestnut Street, A Choice Parcel of the best Spectacles, Microscopes, large and small Pocket Compasses with Dials, and several other sorts of Goods.

Receipt against Heart-Burn
By Benjamin Franklin

The Heart-burn is an uneasy Sensation of Heat in the Stomach, occasioned by Indigestion, which is the Mother of Gout, Rheumatism, Gravel and Stone. To prevent it, Eat no Fat, especially what is burnt or oily; and neither eat or drink any thing sour or acid. To cure it Dissolve a thimble-full of Salt of Wormwood in a Glass of Water, and drink it.

Hell's Kitchen

DEVILLED CRABS

~

PAIN PERDU

~

OYSTERS IN THE HABIT

~

MEDMENHAM À LA MAINTENON

~

BLANC-MANGER ENCORE

"I am in this house much at Ease as if it were my own; and the Gardens are a Paradise. But a pleasanter Thing is the kind Countenance, the facetious and very intelligent Conversation of mine Host, who having been for many Years engaged in publick Affairs, seen all Parts of Europe, and kept the best Company in the World, is himself the best existing."

Benjamin Franklin wrote these words to his son William from the West Wycombe estate of Sir Francis Dashwood (later Lord le Despencer) in August 1773. Franklin had been at West Wycombe before, first in 1772 when he assisted Sir Francis with the Catechism and Psalms in his revision of the Book of Common Prayer. Both Sir Francis and Franklin were Fellows of the Royal Society, where Franklin had dined with him and the 4th Earl of Sandwich when they were Joint Postmasters General.

While staying at West Wycombe in 1773, and always a great campaigner for the American cause, Benjamin Franklin fabricated his famous hoax known as the "King of Prussia Edict", by "Frederick, by the grace of God, King of Prussia, &C. &C. &C." He arranged for a local paper to publish a sham edict in which Frederick proclaimed that Prussia had decided that Britain, having been first settled by the Saxons, was a Prussian colony. Therefore Prussia had the right to raise revenues in the form of taxes in Britain and to ship out all its convicts from Prussian prisons to Britain. These same measures Britain had ordained and commanded from America. As he put it: "And, lastly, being willing farther to favour our said Colonies in Britain, we do hereby also ordain and command, that all the Thieves, highway and street Robbers, House-breakers, Forgers. Murderers, Sodomites, and Villains of every Denomination, who have forfeited their Lives to the Law in Prussia; but whom we, in our great Clemency, do not think fit here to hang, shall be emptied out of our Gaols into the said Island of Great Britain, for the better peopling of that Country." He described his hoax to his son William:

> "I was down at Lord le Despencer's when the Post brought the day's Papers. Paul Whitehead was there too, who runs early through all the Papers and tells the Company what he finds remarkable. He had them in another Room and we were chatting in the breakfast Parlor, when he came running into us, out of breath, with the paper in his hand. 'Here,' he says, 'Here's news for ye. Here's the King of Prussia claiming the Right to this Kingdom.' All stared, and I as much as any body: And he went on to read it. When he had read two or three Paragraphs a Gentleman present said 'Damn his Impudence; I dare say, we shall hear by next Post that he is upon his March with one hundred thousand Men to back this.' Whitehead, who is very shrewd, soon after began to smoke it, and looking in my Face said, 'I'll be hanged if this not some of your American Jokes upon us.' The Reading went on, and ended with abundance of Laughing, and a general Verdict that it was a fair Hit; And the Piece was cut out of the Paper and perserve'd in my Lord's Collection."

Both Sir Francis and Lord Sandwich were "Apostles of the Knights of St Francis of Wycombe", later known as the "Hell-Fire Club", founded in the 1740s by Sir Francis. The twelve club members had their first meetings in the George and Vulture Inn in the City of London, but as the club flourished he found a more secluded meeting place in the ruins of the former Cistercian abbey at Medmenham just six miles west of West Wycombe on the Thames. In the cloisters of the abbey the tables were spread with bottles and "high-relish'd Viands" where the "Mad Monks of Medmenham" enjoyed drinking, good food, and the company of pretty women; happy disciples of Venus and Bacchus:

"No charm has Wine without the Lass: 'Tis Love gives relish to the Glass."

According to the book *Nocturnal Revels* written by one of the monks of that burlesque Order of St Francis and published in 1779: "... every member is allowed to introduce a Lady of a chearful, lively disposition, to improve the general hilarity. Male visitors are also permitted, under certain restrictions; the Master of the Ceremonies, upon this occasion, being their merit, wit, and humour. There is no constraint with regard to the circulation of the glass, after some particular toasts have been given: The Ladies, in the intervals of their repasts, may make select parties among themselves, or entertain one another, or alone, with reading, musick, tambour-work, etc. The salt of these festivities is generally purely Attic, but no indelicacy or indecency is allowed to be intruded without a severe penalty; and a *jeu de mots* must not border too much upon a loose double entendre to be received with applause."

"Homely willing Winn,
With bucksome Bess, and granting Jinn,
All full and plump without, and warm within,
That crackt the bed fast."

Sir Francis and the other chosen twelve sat at the upper table and toasted out of human skulls. The poet Paul Whitehead, who also belonged to the Sublime Society of Beefsteaks, was the High Steward and Treasurer of the Brotherhood, and stood by the side collecting subscriptions from the other friars. His minute book of the gatherings was burnt around 1900 for being too obscene.

The ladies were dressed up like nuns and wore masks. As the poet Charles Churchill put it:

"Whilst Womanhood, in the habit of a Nun
At Mednam lies, by backward Monks undone."

Lord Sandwich, the First Lord of the Admiralty, was unrivalled in the powers of blasphemy, while kneeling down and raising his hands and head towards the heaven, invoking in a perverted phrase of holy writ, those who are to come among them:

"Whilst in most blessed unison, rogue and whore
Clap hands, huzza, and hiccup out, Encore!"

After a silence, the door flung open, and in marched the nuns.
Culinary delights at the club featured such dishes as:

SOUP DE SANTÉ

A soup of beef, knuckle of veal, chicken, bacon, carrots, turnips, onions, mushrooms, lettuce, celery, chervil, and butter. Seasoned with salt, pepper, nutmeg, mace, cloves, parsley and thyme, and thickened with butter and flour.

CARP AU COURT-BOUILLON

Carp poached in water with vinegar, bay leaves, cloves and white pepper; served with a sauce of anchovy, strong gravy, pickled mushroom, thickened with butter and flour.

PUPTON OF PARTRIDGE (OR PIGEON)

Partridge or pigeon baked in a forcemeat-lined dish of veal, chicken, bacon, suet, spinach, mushrooms, parsley, thyme, marjoram, savory and onions; filled with strips of bacon, asparagus tops, mushrooms, hard-boiled egg yolks, cocks' combs, and covered with forcemeat and gravy.

CULLETS À LA MAINE

Chops in melted butter, coated with breadcrumbs, parsley, thyme, savory, nutmeg and mushrooms; baked in greaseproof paper.

BEEF À LA TREMBLADE

Rump of beef with Madeira, onions, cloves, lemon peel, sweet herbs and pepper. Served with sauce of its own stock, chopped onions and parsley, tarragon and lemon juice.

PAIN PERDU

French rolls first stewed in cream and milk, and later fried in clarified butter.

OYSTERS À LA DAUBE

Oysters on the half shell, grilled with parsley, basil, chives, white pepper and white wine.

BLANC-MANGE

Ground almonds simmered in white wine and fish stock, drained and mixed with ground cod, haddock and lobster, simmered in milk and served with roast almonds.

Among its members was the well-known politician John Wilkes, who later supported Benjamin Franklin in the American cause. Wilkes had been prosecuted for sedition; Lord Sandwich played a leading part. There were numerous but unproven rumours of satanism, but the rites they performed were kept strictly secret. As a man of great intelligence, John Wilkes was not afraid of God or man and dismissed the devil as a comic myth. However, he was getting bored with all the satanism at the abbey. During a session at Medmenham, while the friars were donning their cloaks, a gentleman (identifiable as Wilkes), who had availed himself of the office of keeper of the chapel for the occasion, led a great baboon dressed up as the devil into the chapel and shut him up in a chest that stood there to hold ornaments and table utensils. He fastened a cord to the spring of the lock enabling him to open the chest from his seat without being perceived by his fellow friars. When Wilkes pulled the cord, out sprang the baboon onto the table terrifying the monks out of their senses. It then jumped onto the shoulders of Lord Sandwich as he lay sprawling on the floor, who, seeing the animal grinning horribly at him, concluded that the devil had obeyed his summons in good earnest. The more he tried to shake off the baboon, the tighter the creature clung to him, "chattering with spite at his ear" whilst he begged for mercy: "Spare me gracious devil; spare a wretch who never was sincerely your servant! I sinned only from vanity of being in the fashion! Thou knowest I never have been half so wicked as I pretended: never have been able to commit the thousandth part of the vices which I boasted of ... leave me, therefore, and go to those who are more truly devoted to your service. I am but half a sinner."

There is no evidence that Benjamin Franklin took part in the meetings of the Hell-Fire Club, but it is inconceivable that he would have not known about the friars' gatherings at Medmenham Abbey. He was a frequent house guest of Sir Francis and a keen admirer of song, wit, humour and food; it is possible he could have been an occasional participant in the activities of the Knights of St Francis. Especially considering his love of the company of elderly woman, of whom he would say:

"They don't tell
They don't yell
They don't swell
And they're grateful as hell"

Devilled Crabs

3 cups of fresh crab meat ~ 2 eggs ~ 3 tablespoons Dijon mustard
3 tablespoons mayonnaise ~ ½ cup breadcrumbs
½ cup green bell peppers (sweet green peppers), finely chopped
1 small onion finely chopped ~ 1 teaspoon paprika
½ teaspoon Cayenne pepper ~ 1 tablespoon Worcestershire sauce
1 tablespoon vinegar ~ pepper and salt to taste
1 tablespoon finely chopped parsley

Boil eggs until hard, peel them and crumble with a fork. Put the crumbled eggs in a glass bowl and mix in the mustard, vinegar, Worcestershire sauce and mayonnaise until the substance is smooth. Stir in the crabmeat and mix in the breadcrumbs. Blend in the chopped bell peppers, onion and the Cayenne pepper, salt and pepper. Fill the crab shells with the mixture and dust with paprika and finely chopped parsley and bake in a preheated oven at 350°F (gas mark 4) for 15–20 minutes, or until brown.

Pain Perdu

"Having two French rolls, cut them into slices as thick as your Finger, crumb and crust together, lay them on a Dish, put to them a Pint of Cream and Half a Pint of Milk. Stew them over with beaten Cinnamon and Sugar, turn them frequently till they are tender, but take care not to break them. Then take them from the cream with a slice, break four or five Eggs, and fry them in clarified Butter. Make them of a good brown Colour, but not black. Scrape a little sugar on them. They may be served for a second Course Dish, but fittest for Supper."

Oysters in the Habit

1 dozen oysters ~ 4 oz butter ~ ½ cup dry white wine
3 small bread rolls ~ 1 teaspoon nutmeg ~ 1 teaspoon mace
1 teaspoon salt ~ 1 teaspoon pepper ~ 3 dashes Tabasco

Toast the rolls lightly in the oven. Sauté the oysters in butter with nutmeg, mace, salt and pepper. Pour in the wine with the Tabasco and reduce. Hollow the rolls and stuff them with the sautéed oysters. Put back into a 375°F oven (gas mark 5) for 20 minutes. (In the 18th century these stuffed rolls were deep fried in lard before being eaten.)

Medmenham à la Maintenon

"Cut your Cutlets handsomely, beat them thin with your Cleaver, season them with Pepper and Salt. Make a Force-meat with Veal, Beef Sewet, Spice and sweet Herbs, roll'd in Yolks of Eggs. Roll Force-meat round each Cutlet within two Inches of the Top of the Bone, then have as many Half Sheets of white Paper as Cutlets. Roll each Cutlet in a piece of Paper, first buttering the Paper well on the Inside. Dip the Cutlets in melt'd Butter and then in Crumbs of Bread. Lay each Cutlet on half a sheet of Paper cross the Middle of it, leaving about an Inch of Bone out. Then close the two Ends of your Paper as you do a Turnover Tart, and cut off the Paper that is too much. Broil your Mutton Cutlets Half and Hour, your Veal Cutlets three Quarters of an Hour."

"If thou art dull and heavy after Meat, it's a sign thou hast exceeded the due Measure; for Meat and Drink ought to refresh the Body, and make it cheerful, and not to dull and oppress it." BENJAMIN FRANKLIN

[38]

Blanc-Manger Encore

4 oz white almonds ~ 1½ oz cornflour ~ 3 tablespoons fine sugar
1 pint milk ~ 2 teaspoons orange zest

Take the skinned almonds and crush them fine with a pestle and mortar. Blend with the cornflour and 3 tablespoons of milk until you get a smooth paste. Put the remaining milk with the orange rind in a saucepan and bring to the boil. Strain the milk onto the blended paste and stir well all the time. Return the new mixture to the saucepan and bring back to the boil. Add the fine sugar and stir well until it thickens. Boil for another 3–4 minutes. Pour the mixture into a wet mould and leave to cool for several hours until it is set. Turn it out on a serving platter and serve with peeled orange wedges.

[SANDWICHES]

John Montague, 4th Earl of Sandwich (1718–92), was an inveterate gambler who would order cold meat between two slices of bread to be brought to him so that he did not have to leave the gambling table at meal times. The sandwich was named after him.

[MUSTARD]

Crushed black mustard seeds were used in biblical times, when they were imported from Palestine into Egypt and there used as a condiment. Later the Greeks and Romans ground the seeds into a powder, which was then used to spice up gravies for meat and fish. During the Middle Ages mustard seeds were valued for their medicinal qualities. Pope John XXII, the most celebrated Avignon pope was known to be a lover of mustard and even had his nephew instated as Official Mustard Supplier to the Papacy. The city of Orleans in France was the first to manufacture mustard by blending the seeds with vinegar in the late 16th century. And later, in the 18th century, Dijon started the concoction of white mustard in which the black seeds were blended with white grape juice and white wine.

❦ ❦ ❦

THE PENNSYLVANIA GAZETTE, 6 April. 1732

Advertisement

Choice Flour of Mustard-Seed, in Bottles, very convenient for such as go to Sea; to a little of which if you put hot Water, and stop it up close, you will have strong Mustard, fir to use, in 15 minutes. Sold at the New Printing-Office near the Market, at 1s. per Bot.

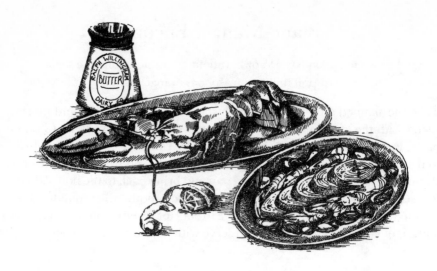

Pesca Vegetarian

STUFFED LOBSTER

~

BLOCK ISLAND COD STEAKS

~

CORN OYSTERS

~

QUINCE PUDDING

~

MADEIRA WINE

After quarrels with his older brother in 1723, Benjamin Franklin decided to leave Boston and assert his own freedom. Very much against the wishes of his father the seventeen-year-old Benjamin Franklin left Boston for New York, where he offered his services to a printer Mr William Bradford. Bradford could not give him employment, but suggested he go on to Philadelphia where his son had lost his principal hand. Philadelphia was 100 miles farther. Later in his autobiography Benjamin writes:

> I believe I have omitted mentioning that in my first Voyage from Boston, being becalm'd off Block Island, our People set about catching Cod, and hauled up a great many. Hitherto I had stuck to my Resolution of not eating animal Food; and on this Occasion, I consider'd, with my Master Tryon, the taking of every Fish as a kind of unprovoked Murder, since none of them had or ever could do us any Injury that might justify the Slaughter. All this seemed very reasonable. But

I had formerly been a great lover of Fish, and when this came hot out of the frying-pan, it smelt admirably well. I balanc'd some time between Principle and Inclination; till I recollected, that when the Fish were opened, I saw smaller Fish taken out of their Stomachs: Then thought I, if you eat one another, I don't see why we mayn't eat you. So I din'd upon Cod very heartily, and continued to eat with other People, returning only now and then occasionally to a vegetable Diet. So convenient a Thing it is to be a reasonable creature, since it enables one to find or make a Reason for every thing one has a Mind to do.

Stuffed Lobster

1 medium lobster ~ 2 cups breadcrumbs ~ ½ cup melted butter
1 teaspoon Dijon mustard ~ 1 teaspoon salt ~ 1 teaspoon pepper
1 teaspoon Cayenne pepper ~ 2 tablespoons lemon juice

Boil the lobster by picking up a live one and letting it slide into a large pan of briskly boiling water. Boil for about 10 minutes. Drain the lobster and let it cool off. Split the back open, take the meat out and clean the inside. Mix the lobster meat in a glass bowl into a stuffing with the breadcrumbs, melted butter, lemon juice, Dijon mustard, salt, pepper and Cayenne pepper. Spoon the stuffing back into the lobster shell and bake in a preheated 375°F (gas mark 5) oven for 30 minutes. Serve with more melted butter.

Block Island Cod Steaks

4 cod steaks ~ ½ pint soured cream ~ 1 teaspoon salt ~ 1 teaspoon pepper
2 cups red seedless grapes ~ 4 large sprigs of tarragon

Season cod steaks with salt and pepper. Put them in a shallow dish and cover with soured cream and tarragon sprigs. Preheat the oven at 450°F (gas mark 8) and bake for 10–15 minutes, or until the steaks are just cooked on the inside. Blanch the grapes in water and peel them. Take the cod steaks out of the oven, pour the juices in a sauté pan, and add some more soured cream until it thickens. Arrange the steaks onto a serving platter and pour the thick white sauce over the steaks. Dress them up with the peeled red grapes.

"A Countryman between 2 Lawyers is like a Fish between two Cats"
BENJAMIN FRANKLIN

Corn Oysters

2 cups of corn kernels, fresh off the ears
2 tablespoons flour ~ 2 eggs, beaten ~ 1 teaspoon salt
1 teaspoon pepper

Mix the flour with the corn kernels thoroughly, and add salt and pepper and the beaten eggs in order to create a thick consistency. When too thin, just add some more flour. Roll into small oyster-shaped little lumps and arrange them in a deep-fryer. Fry in fresh hot oil.

"Eat to live, and not live to eat"   BENJAMIN FRANKLIN

Quince Pudding

"Scald your Quinces very tender, pare them very thin, scrape off the soft. Mix it with Sugar very sweet, put in a little Ginger and a little Cinnamon. To a Pint of Cream, you must put three or four Yolks of Eggs, and stir it into your Quinces till they are of good Thickness. It must be pretty thick. Butter your Dish, pour it in and bake it."

Madeira Wine

On June 2, 1765, Benjamin Franklin wrote in a letter from Craven Street to Lord Kames:

"… You require my History from the time I set Sail for America. I left England about the End of August 1762, in Company with Ten Sail of Merchant Ships under Convoy of a Man of War. We had a pleasant Passage to Madeira, an Island and Colony belonging to Portugal, where we were kindly receiv'd and entertain'd, our Nation being then in high Honour with them, on Account of the Protection it was at that time affording their Mother Country from the united Invasions of France and Spain. 'Tis a fertile Island, and the different Heights and Situations among its Mountains, afford such different Temperaments of Air, that all the Fruits of Northern and southern Countries are produc'd there, Corn, Grapes, Apples, Peaches, Oranges, Lemons, Plantains, Bananas, &c. Here we furnish'd ourselves with fresh Provisions and Refreshments of all kinds, and after a few Days proceeded on our Voyage, running Southward till we got into the Trade Winds, and then with them Westward till we drew near the Coast of America."

On February 25, 1779, Benjamin Franklin wrote in a letter from Passy to John Bondfield:

"I think our People mad to give such a Price for Madeira. I hope the Bordeaux you send will be so good as to alter their Taste."

"You will say my Advice smell'd of Madeira. You are right. This foolish Letter is mere chit-chat between ourselves, over the second Bottle"

BENJAMIN FRANKLIN

[MADEIRA]

The Madeira Islands were known to the Romans, but rediscovered in the 15th century by Prince Henry the Navigator of Portugal where he instigated the development of the vineyards and where the climate and soil were ideal for production of wine. Madeira's geographical situation made it easy for ships to carry the wines to other parts of the world. By the end of the 15th century Madeira wines were quite popular in France and England. In the 17th century it was King Charles II of England who forbade the importation of any other wine to the American colonies, except Madeira. In 1662 he married Catherine of Braganza of Portugal, who held a wealthy dowry, which might even have included Madeira. This edict was to last for about 100 years. It was not surprising then that Madeira wines became popular in America and were the favourites of George Washington, Thomas Jefferson and Benjamin Franklin. In 1768 the sloop *Liberty*, which was owned by John Hancock, tried to smuggle a cargo of Madeira and other wines into Boston Harbour. The wines were destined for Hancock himself, but the shipment was intercepted by the English. Hancock put up a fierce fight, being defended by the lawyer John Adams and finally received his precious Madeira wines. This successful "Boston Madeira Party" was to be repeated five years later, in 1773. This time the cargo was going to be tea. It is said that at the signing of the Declaration of Independence in 1776 a toast was made by the delegates with Madeira wine. Early in the 19th century during the Napoleonic occupation of Spain and Portugal, when France tried to blockade the sea route to Madeira, the stockpiles on the island started to build up and the fear arose that the wine was going to go to waste. This was when, in desperation to preserve the wine, it was blended with brandy. This process of fortification was very successful and further enhanced the taste of the wine. A mildew epidemic in 1852 and a vine pest in 1873 had disastrous consequences; the old wine reserves for blending were soon depleted, leading to a drop in quality of the wine.

Benjamin's Stoves

JUMPING FROM FEET TO EARS

~

SAUTÉED CHICKEN AND BROCCOLI

~

SUCKLING PIG

~

APPLE PUDDING

~

HOT RUM GROG

At home in Philadelphia, Benjamin Franklin invented the Pennsylvania Fireplace, later known as the Franklin Stove. An ingenious piece of engineering, it burnt wood economically, radiated the heat and reduced smoke and draft. He took the fireplace out into the room, and made it out of iron. It had a device that separated the smoke from the heat. The smoke could rise up the chimney, while the heat went into the room.

Benjamin Franklin, in his discourse explaining his new invention, describes the type of fireplaces until then:

1. The large open Fire-places used in the Days of our Fathers, and still generally in the Country, and in Kitchens.

2. The newer-fashion'd Fire-places, with low Breasts, and narrow Hearths.

3. Fire-places with hollow Backs, Hearths and Jams of Iron, for warming the Air as it comes into the Room.

4. The Holland Stoves, with Iron Doors opening into the Room.

5. The German Stoves, which have no Opening in the Room where they are us'd, but the Fire is put in from some other Room or from without.

6. Iron Pots, with open Charcoal Fires, plac'd in the middle of a Room.

This new invention was meticulously described in what one now could call a "promotional brochure" and advertized in *The Pennsylvania Gazette*:

JUST PUBLISHED

An account of the New-Invented Pennsylvania Fire-Places: Wherein their Construction and Manner of Operation is particularly explained; their Advantages above every other Method of warming Rooms demonstrated; and all Objections that have been raised against the Use of them answered and obviated. With Directions for putting them up, and for using them to the best Advantage. And a Copper-Plate, in which the several Parts of the Machine are exactly laid down, from a Scale of equal Parts. Price 1s.

Benjamin Franklin's brochure brought him many customers, even the Governor of Pennsylvania, of whom Franklin said:

"Governor Thomas was so pleas'd with the Construction of his Stove, that he offer'd to give me a Patent for the sole Vending of them for a Term of Years; but I declin'd it from a Principle which has ever weigh'd with me on such Occasions, viz. That as we enjoy great Advantages from the Inventions of others, we should be glad of an Opportunity to serve others by any Invention of ours, and this we should do freely and generously."

Later in London he had his fireplace installed at his lodgings in Craven Street. And it was in London that Benjamin Franklin discovered an iron-monger who had made a few changes to his fireplace specifications, and was granted a patent. The ironmonger made, as Franklin put it: "a little Fortune by it."

In 1776 there was a gentleman called Benjamin Thompson from Massachusetts, later Count Rumford of the Holy Roman Empire, who sided with the British during the American Revolution, and moved to Europe. This Benjamin brought his own revolution about by designing 18th century cooking ranges. Till then cooking had taken place in the fireplace and Thompson transferred it to the stove; a range with an oven below. Stoves had been in use for many years, but now they started to be used for cooking. With the new range came the invention of the sauté pan, which could be put on the stove and used for making all kinds of delicious sauces; a pan out of which the fat could 'jump' (*sauter* in French).

Jumping from Feet to Ears

2 lbs hog's ears ~ 1 hog's trotter ~ 1 large onion, finely chopped
½ cup of flour ~ 6 tablespoons butter ~ ½ cup flour ~ 2 cups gravy
3 teaspoons salt ~ 3 teaspoons pepper ~ 1 tablespoon mustard
1 tablespoon vinegar

Boil the pig's trotter in salted water. Slice the pig's ears thinly. Make a *roux* with the butter and flour and sauté the chopped onion in the *roux*. Moisten with some gravy. Put in the ears and season with pepper and salt. Simmer until the onion and strips of ear are cooked and the *ragoût* thickens. Pour in some vinegar and add the mustard and reheat. When the pig's trotter is done, put it onto a serving dish and arrange the *ragoût* of ears around it. So, "have ready your feet, split, crumb'd and boil'd to lay around your ears".

"Anger warms the Invention, but overheats the Oven"
BENJAMIN FRANKLIN

Sautéed Chicken and Broccoli

1 lb boneless and quartered chicken thighs
1 lb broccoli heads with trimmed stems ~ 1 cup quartered tomatoes
1 cup finely chopped onion ~ 2 tablespoons chopped garlic
4 tablespoons olive oil ~ 1 tablespoon finely chopped ginger
1 teaspoon ground black pepper ~ 1 teaspoon salt
2 teaspoons of mixed herbs ~ 3 tablespoons Worcestershire sauce
2 teaspoons chopped chilli peppers ~ 1 cup chicken stock

Combine chicken pieces with pepper, salt, Worcestershire sauce and Tabasco. Heat olive oil in sauté pan till hot and sauté chicken pieces until golden brown. Remove chicken from pan and drain. Reheat pan. Add 1 tablespoon of olive oil and add onion, garlic and ginger for 1 minute. Add broccoli pieces and sauté for 2 minutes. Add chicken stock, mixed herbs and tomatoes. Continue to sauté at moderate heat for 4 minutes. Add drained chicken to mixture till chicken is thoroughly reheated and serve at once.

Chicken Stock

1 raw or cooked chicken carcass ~ 2 bay leaves ~ 3 shallots
the giblets of the bird ~ 2 pints of water ~ ½ cup of dry white wine
1 teaspoon white peppercorns ~ 1 teaspoon coarse salt

Break up the bones of the carcass, either with a hammer or a nutcracker, to extract most of the nutritional goodness. Chop the shallots coarsely. Slide the cracked bones into the water and add the dry white wine, the bay leaves, the chopped shallots, the giblets and the white peppercorns and coarse salt. Bring the water quickly to a boil. Remove any scum, cover and simmer for at least 2 hours. Strain the stock and discard the bones and vegetables.

Suckling Pig

"Before placing the Suckling Pig in front of the Fire, take a some very finely chopped Sage, a Piece of Butter as large as a Walnut, and a bit of Pepper and Salt. Put these inside the Pig and sew it up with large thread. Sprinkle it entirely with Flour and keep on sprinkling until the Eyes drop or the Skin is well browned. Make sure to catch all the Juices that drip from the Pig in Bowls or Pipkins which you should place in a Dripping-pan below.

"When the Pig is well-roasted, light a bright Fire, take a clean Cloth and put in there a quadroon of Butter and rub the Pig with it, until the Skin is perfectly brown. Take next the Pig from the Fire, place it on a Platter, and cut the Head off, and cut the Pig in half before pulling it off the Spit.

"At that time, cut off the Ears place one at every end of the Platter, and also the Jaw below and put it on one side. Melt some fresh Butter, take the kept Juices and add them to the Butter, bring this to a boil, pour it onto the Platter with the Pig's Brains, cut into pieces and mixed with the Sage, and put it on the Table."

Apple Pudding

"Make a puff-paste dough. Roll it out until it's half a thumb thick. Peel your apples and cut them into pieces in an enough quantity to fill the crust, place them in it. Put everything in a cloth and boil it for two hours to make a small pudding, and for three to four hours to make a large one. When it is well cooked, place it on your platter, cut a piece off the crust and add some butter and sugar to taste. Put back the cut-off piece and serve it hot on the table. To make a pear pudding, do it in the same way. You can likewise make a damson pudding or that from any other kind of plums. From apricots, cherries, or from blackberries and they are very sweet".

Puff-Paste

"Take a quarter of a peck [4 pints] of flour, rub fine half a pound of butter, a little salt, make it up into a light paste with cold water, just stiff enough to work it well up; then roll it out, and stick pieces of butter all over, and strew a little flour; roll it up, and roll it out again; and so do nine or ten times, till you have rolled in a pound and a half of butter. This crust is mostly used for all sorts of pies."

A peck is a measure of dry goods equivalent to 2 imperial gallons.

Hot Rum Grog

Benjamin Franklin participated in an expedition from Bethlehem to Gnadenhutten in 1756, to choose a place where to build Fort Allen, north of the Blue Mountains in Pennsylvania. The purpose of the expedition was to find suitable place to build forts as protection against Indian attacks. The fort was going to be about 125 feet long and 50 feet wide. They had regular prayers in the morning and evening. Benjamin Franklin commented on the attendance of the services:

"We had for our chaplain a zealous Presbyterian Minister, Mr Beatty, who explain'd to me that the Men did not generally attend his Prayers and Exhortations. When they enlisted, they were promis'd, besides Pay and Provisions, a Gill of Rum a Day, which was punctually serv'd out to them half in the Morning and the other half in the Evening, and I observ'd they were as punctual in attending to receive it. Upon which I said to Mr Beatty, 'It is perhaps below the Dignity of your Profession to act as Steward of the Rum. But if you were to deal it out, and only just after Prayers, you would have them all about you.' He lik'd the Thought, undertook the Office, and with the help of a few hands to measure out the Liquor executed it to satisfaction; and never were Prayers more generally and more punctually attended. So that I thought this Method preferable to the Punishments inflicted by some military Laws for Non-Attendance on Divine Service."

½ pint dark rum ~ 2 oz orange juice ~ 2 oz lemon juice
4 oz honey ~ ½ teaspoon ground cinnamon ~ ½ teaspoon ground cloves
½ teaspoon ground ginger

Pour the rum, lemon and orange juice in a saucepan and heat gently until simmering. Add the honey, cinnamon, cloves and ginger. Simmer for 10 minutes and serve in a glass.

[CHILLI]

The Chilli pepper originates in the jungles of the Amazon River and its seeds were spread by the Amazon and Aztecs Indians throughout the continent into Mexico during the pre-Hispanic period. There are Aztec recipes 2,000 years old, where hot chillies are added to stews. The chilli was also a tributary product. Conquered tribes had to pay tribute to the sovereign, mostly being loads of food products such as beans, corn and chilli. The tribute depended on the product; chilli was either delivered daily, weekly or monthly (20 days in an Aztec month), every 80 days (4 months), or once a year. The loads were the equivalent of what a carrier could carry on his back. When Christopher Columbus arrived in the Americas, thinking he had reached the Indies, he mistakenly took chillies for peppercorns and called them "peppers". In the 18th century the Brazilian Jesuit priest Francisco Clavijero, who was born in Vera Cruz, Mexico, wrote that the chilli pepper was to the Mexicans what salt was to the Europeans. It was during the early 1800s when British settlers came to Texas, that they wanted to duplicate curry powder, when they mixed dried garlic, oregano and chilli peppers and ground them in a mortar. This was when chilli powder came into its existence. During the Gold Rush prospectors took "chilli bricks" along with them on their trek to California. These were compressed bricks made of beef with lard and chilli peppers that could be heated on the trail and mixed with any vegetables gathered en route.

[GROG]

The British Admiral Edward Vernon was nicknamed the "Old Grog" for introducing a rum drink diluted with water, in 1740. He was in the habit of wearing a grogram or cloak, hence the origin of the well-known hot drink.

THE PENNSYLVANIA GAZETTE, Dec. 3. 1741

Advertisement

To be sold at the Post Office Philadelphia, the New Invented Fire-Places; Where any Person may see some of them that are now in Use, and have the Nature and Advantages of them explain'd.

> ANOTHER Sun! — 'tis true; —but not THE SAME.
> Alike, I own, in Warmth and genial Flame:
> But, more obliging than his elder Brother,
> This will not scorch in Summer, like the other;
> Nor, when sharp Boreas chills our shiv'ring Limbs,
> Will this Sun leave us for more Southern Climes;
> Or, in long Winter Nights, forsake us here,
> To chear new Friends in t'other Hemisphere:
> But, faithful still to us, this new Sun's Fire,
> Warms when we please, and just as we desire.

Receipt for the Dry-Grips (dry flu)
By Benjamin Franklin

Take sixty Drops of Tincture of Castor, thirty of liquid Laudanum, in an Ounce of Mint or simple Water, sweetened to your Taste; take of this Mixture a Spoonful every Half Hour, till you find relief.

These Remedies are said to be excellent in their Kind; but as a Case may be mistaken by the Unskilful, let me, tho' no Physician, prescribe something more, viz. Whenever you can have the Advice of a skilful Physician, Take that.

Passy Passion

POTAGE AU DIPLOMAT FRANKLIN

~

SAUMON FROID À LA COMTESSE D'HOUDETOT

~

TIMBALE DE VOLAILLE À LA BRILLANTE

~

SORBETS AU VIN DE CHAMPAGNE

~

JAMBON À LA PASSY, POUR RELÈVE

~

CÔTELETTES D'AGNEAU À LA DAME D'AUTEUIL, AUX POINTES
D'ASPERGE

~

MACÉDOINE DE LÉGUMES

~

MERINGUES DU ROI

Benjamin Franklin's life at Passy from 1777 was one of public modesty and private affluence. His breakfasts comprised bread and butter, honey, coffee or his favourite tea. For dinner there were hors d'œuvres, joints of beef, mutton or veal. Game and fowl were served as well as his beloved vegetables, and there were pastries, sweets, compotes, and various kinds of fruit.

"I think the French cookery agrees with me better than the English; I suppose because there is little or no butter in their sauces; for I have never once had the heartburn since my being here though I eat heartily, which shows that my digestion is good."

There were cheeses, biscuits and ices and there were also wines from his well-stocked wine cellar. He drank red or white Bordeaux and Champagne. There was sparkling wine and *vin ordinaire* for his nine servants. He also kept several dozen bottles of rum and of his much loved Madeira. One of Franklin's French critics, however, wrote about his bad table manners, complaining he "bit off the heads of the asparagus, instead of using a fork, and broke his eggs in a cup, making a 'philosophical ragoût' with eggs, butter, mustard, pepper, and salt, like the 'kind of savage' he was".

An inventory in February 1779 of Franklin's wine cellar in Passy recorded the following:

Etat du Vin dans la Cave Fevrier 1. 1779	Bouteilles
Vin de chairaisse (sherry)	148
Vin rouge de Bordeaux venue dans des Caises	85
Vin blanc de Bordeaux venue dans des Caises	34
Vin rouge de Bordeaux l'année 1761	15
Vin rouge de Bordeaux mis en bouteille à Passy	159
Vin blanc de Champagne venue dans des Caises	21
Vin blanc de Champagne mousseu	326
Vin de Bourgogne rouge	113
Vin rouge d'ordinaire	209
Vin blanc d'ordinaire	10
Vin inconnu demi bouteille	12
Rum	48
Eau de vie d'Andaille	58
1 Piece (barrel) de Bordeaux rouge	
2 Pieces Vins ordinaire.	

In France Benjamin Franklin surrounded himself with women of great social standing. He formally befriended the comtesse d'Houdetot, whom Rousseau had loved unrequitedly, and the duchesse d'Anville, the mother of the duc de la Rochefoucauld. Closer to home in Passy he forged much more intimate friendships with Madame Brillon de Jouy and with Madame Helvétius, widow of the renowned philosopher.

Comtesse d'Houdetot invited "mon cher et vénérable Docteur" Franklin to plant an acacia tree during a country feast in his honour at her husband's château. From a very early age she had been a great lover of poetry. When Franklin arrived at the château, comtesse d'Houdetot had gone out onto the road to meet him in his carriage and recited to him:

> Spirit of a hero and a wise man
> O Liberty, first benefit of the gods

Inside the château he was feasted on a splendid banquet accompanied by lots of poetry. Each guest with glass in hand sang poems to him and Franklin raised his glass in turn. After dinner when he planted the acacia tree, the comtesse d'Houdetot had arranged for an orchestra to play music and a chorus to sing in honour of his lightning rod. The evening was brought to a climax when Franklin climbed back into his carriage and the comtesse recited:

> Legislator of one world, and benefactor of both,
> A man who always deserves his respects;
> And I shall receive in those places
> The debt of all times.

Madame Brillon was Franklin's favourite and it is said he spent two evenings a week with her, when she gave concerts and served tea. He nicknamed her "La Brillante" and about her home he said: "I call this my Opera, for I go rarely to the Opera in Paris." Madame Brillon, who was in her thirties, while Franklin was in his seventies, loved to sit on his lap and hug and kiss him. She told him that in French it was always very good to say: "Je vous aime," and added: "Leave grammar to the academicians."

In a letter Benjamin Franklin waxed eloquent about French ladies:

"This is the civilest Nation upon Earth. Your first Acquaintances endeavour to find out what you are like, and they tell others. If 'tis understood that you like Mutton, dine where you will find Mutton. Somebody, it seems, gave it out that I lov'd Ladies; and then every body presented me their Ladies (or the Ladies presented themselves) to be embrac'd , that is to have their Necks kiss'd. For as to kissing the Lips or Cheeks it is not the Mode here, the first is reckon'd rude, & the other may rub off the Paint. The French Ladies have however 1000 other ways of rendering themselves agreable; by their various Attentions and Civilities, & their sensible Conversation. 'Tis a delightful People to live with."

And as Madame Brillon could only add:

> Always love God, America
> and above all myself.

With the more aristocratic Madame Helvétius, who lived in neighbouring Auteuil, Benjamin Franklin had a different kind of relationship. She absolutely fascinated him and soon he had given her the name "Notre Dame d'Auteuil". It was not long before he had fallen in love with her and begun having notes sent to her. One morning Madame Helvétius invited Benjamin Franklin and his grandson Temple for breakfast at home where they arrived on foot and very late:

"As the invitation was for eleven o'Clock I expected to find a Breakfast in the manner of a Dinner; that there would be many Guests; that we should have not only Tea, but also Coffee, Chocolate, perhaps a Ham and several other good things. I resolved to go there on foot. My Shoes were a little too tight. I arrived almost crippl'd. On entering the Courtyard, I was a little surprised to find it so empty of Carriages, and to see that we were the first to arrive. We went upstairs. No noise at all. We went into the Dining Room. No one except M. l'Abbe (Morelett) and Mr C. Breakfast finish'd and eaten! Nothing on the Table except some Morsels of Bread and a little Butter. They exclaim; they run to tell Madame Helvetius that we had come for Breakfast. She leaves her Toilette, and comes with her hair half-comb'd. They are surprised that I have come ... Finally another Breakfast is order'd. One of them runs for fresh Water, another for Coal. They blow vigorously to make a Fire. I was very hungry; it was so late; 'A watch'd Pot never boils', as Poor Richard says. Madame departs for Paris, leaving us. We begin to eat. The Butter is soon finish'd. Monsieur l'Abbe asks if we want some more? Yes, certainly. He rings. No one comes. We chat. He forgets the Butter. I was scraping the Plate; then he seizes it and runs to the Kitchen, looking for some. After a while, he returns slowly, saying sadly: there is none in the House. In order to entertain me, Monsieur l'Abbe proposes a Walk. My Feet will not allow it. Consequently, we leave Breakfast there and go up to his Room in order to find something with which to finish our Repast – his good Books."

John and Abigail Adams came to France in 1778 and were warmly greeted by Franklin. He introduced them to his friends and tried to make them feel at home. However, John Adams was not amused; he found Franklin's lifestyle extravagant. And when the Adams were invited to dine with Franklin at Madame Helvétius's in Auteuil, it was the first time the Puritan Abigail had met the worldy Madame Helvétius. She could not believe the decadent moralities of the French, and later wrote thus about Madame Helvétius:

She entered the room with a careless, jaunty air; upon seeing the ladies who were strangers to her, she bawled out, 'Ah! Mon Dieu, where is Franklin? Why did you not tell me there were ladies here?' You must suppose her speaking all this in French. 'How I look!' said she, taking hold of a chemise of tiffany, which she had on over a blue lutestring, and which looked as much upon decay as her beauty, for she was once a handsome woman. Her hair was frizzled; over it she had a small straw hat, with as dirty gauze half-handkerchief behind. She had a black gauze scarf over her shoulders. She ran out of the room; when she returned, the Doctor entered at one door, she at the other; upon which she ran forward to him and caught him by the hand, 'Helas, Franklin!' then gave him a double kiss, one upon each cheek, and another upon his forehead. When we went into the room to dine, she was placed between the Doctor and Mr Adams. She carried on the chief of the conversation at dinner, frequently locking her hands into the Doctor's, and sometimes spreading her arms upon the backs of both the gentlemen's chairs, then throwing her arms carelessly upon the Doctor's neck. I should have been greatly astonished at this conduct, if the good Doctor had not told me that in this lady I should see a genuine Frenchwoman, wholly free from affectation or stiffness of behavior, and one of the best women in the world. I own

Sèvres soft-paste porcelain cup and saucer (*gobelet litron et soucoupe*) with a dark blue (*bleu nouveau*) ground, gilding and enamel "jewels", *circa* 1785. With cameo-style painted portraits of Louis XVI, Marie-Antoinette, Frederick the Great of Prussia, the Queen of Prussia and of Benjamin Franklin. (Private Collection, USA, courtesy of Adrian Sassoon)

I was highly disgusted, and never wish for an acquaintance with ladies of her cast. After dinner, she threw herself on a settee, where she showed more than her feet. She had a little lap-dog, who was, next to the Doctor, her favorite. This she kissed, and when he wet the floor she wiped it up with her chemise. This is one of the Doctor's most intimate friends, with whom he dines once every week, and she with him.

Benjamin Franklin later on proposed marriage to Madame Helvétius, but she rejected him. He went back to Passy and wrote his most famous bagatelles, called "The Elysian Fields", in which he wrote:

"Sadden'd by your barbarous Resolution, stated so positively last Night, to remain single the rest of your Life, in honor of your dead Husband, I went home, fell on my Bed, believing myself dead, and found myself in the Elysian Fields."

In the summer of 1785 when "le diplomat" was en route to Le Havre on his way back to Philadelphia, in a litter borrowed from the French queen,

[55]

Madame Helvétius sent him one last message by road: "I picture you in the litter, farther from us at every step, already lost to me and to those who loved you so much and regret you so. I fear you are in pain … If you are, come back, mon cher ami, come back to us!"

Departing from Le Havre on July 19, 1785, he wrote a final letter to his "Dame d'Auteuil", ending it thus: "I am not telling you that I love you. I would be told that there is nothing extraordinary and no merit at all in that, because everyone loves you. I only hope that you will always love me a little."

Many of Benjamin Franklin's friends; the chemist Lavoisier, the mayor of Paris Bailly, the duc de la Rochefoucauld and the mayor of Passy, did not survive the upcoming French Revolution. They were all guillotined, as was the man whose name is linked to the enlightened instrument of death, Docteur Guillotin. Madame Helvétius, however, survived the hounding and execution of the aristocracy and wisely buried her precious worldly treasures in her very own garden in Auteuil.

Potage au diplomat Franklin

1 lb rump beef ~ 6 pints *consommé à l'anglaise* ~ 2 cups Madeira
1 teaspoon Cayenne pepper ~ 2 cups Merlot wine
1 cup shredded leftover dark pheasant meat

Consommé à l'anglaise

2 lbs shin beef ~ 1 veal knuckle ~ 1 slab of raw ham
2 lbs pieces of poultry (bones, wings, legs)
2 lbs pieces of shoulder of lamb ~ 8 oz carrots, sliced
8 oz turnips, sliced ~ 4 oz celery, sliced ~ 4 oz red onions, quartered
4 oz leek, sliced ~ 4 bay leaves ~ 3 sprigs of parsley
2 sprigs of thyme ~ 1 teaspoon cloves ~ 1 tablespoon salt
1 tablespoon crushed black pepper ~ 8 pints of water

Put beef, veal, ham, poultry, and lamb into the water and bring to a soft boil. Add salt, pepper, bay leaves, and cloves. Add all the vegetables and bring back to a boil. Reduce heat and simmer for 2–3 hours, constantly skimming off the scum, stirring from time to time. Simmer for another 2–3 hours (total cooking time 5–6 hours). Strain the stock first through a colander and then through a sieve. Cover the stock with a lid and let it cool off. Refrigerate overnight and scoop off the solid fat from the surface.

To prepare the potage; cut the rump beef in thin strips, hit them with a meat pouncer till flat. Trim them into new strips, about 1 inch long. Put the strips of beef in a casserole and add the Madeira wine. Add the prepared *consommé à l'anglaise* to the beef and Madeira and bring to a slow boil. Reduce heat and add Cayenne pepper, Merlot wine and the shredded pheasant meat. Bring back to a boil, then back to simmer for 20 minutes or till the strips of beef are cooked.

Saumon froid à la comtesse d'Houdetot

2 lbs salmon ~ ½ lb shrimps ~ hard-boiled eggs ~ *sauce tartare*

The court-bouillon

1 carrot ~ 1 onion ~ 2 sticks of celery ~ 2 shallots ~ 2 bay leaves
3 sprigs of parsley ~ 2 sprigs of thyme ~ 3 tablespoons lemon juice
½ pint of dry white wine ~ salt and pepper

Make *court-bouillon* by bringing 2 pints of water to a boil with the carrots, onion, celery, shallots, bay leaves, parsley, thyme, salt and pepper, lemon juice and the dry white wine. Let simmer for 20 minutes.

The sauce tartare

2 egg yolks ~ 1 teaspoon salt ~ 1 teaspoon ground white pepper
2 teaspoons Dijon mustard ~ 3 teaspoons lemon juice ~ 6 fl oz olive oil
1 tablespoon finely-chopped *cornichons* ~ 2 teaspoons capers
1 tablespoon chopped green olives
1 large finely-chopped spring onion (scallion)

First make a mayonnaise by whisking together egg yolks, salt, pepper, mustard in a glass mixing bowl. Slowly whisk in the lemon juice. Then add the olive oil drop by drop while whisking continuously until the mayonnaise starts to thicken. Keep on adding the olive oil until it is all whisked in. If the substance becomes too thick, stir in some warm water until you have the right consistency. Stir in the chopped *cornichons*, capers, chopped green olives and spring onion (scallions).

Put salmon in a fish kettle, pour the *court-bouillon* over it and bring first to a boil and then simmer for 25 minutes. Lift salmon out of kettle and leave to cool for 2½ hours. Remove skin and dark meat, so that only the pink flesh remains. Garnish with cooked and peeled shrimps, and slices of hard-boiled egg. Serve with the *sauce tartare*. Garnish with sprigs of parsley.

Timbale de volaille "à la Brillante"

1 lb roasted mallard duck breast ~ 2 tablespoons flour ~ 6 oz butter
3 cups sautéed mushrooms ~ 4 tablespoons port
1 lb veal forcemeat ~ 3 oz black truffles ~ 8 oz *foie gras*

Butter a pie dish generously, decorate the bottom and all sides with pieces of truffle and apply a ½-inch layer of veal forcemeat. Make a *roux* with flour and butter and gradually add the port, until you have a thick sauce. Add the pieces of duck breast and 1 cup of the sautéed mushrooms and make a thick *ragoût*. Fill the rest of the pie dish up with the *ragoût* of duck pieces and the remaining 2 cups of sautéed mushrooms. Seal the pie dish with another layer of forcemeat. Finally, cover with a piece of greaseproof paper and stand the dish in a casserole containing water to about a quarter of the dish's height. Poach the dish *au bain-marie*. When serving, remove the greaseproof paper and pour off some of the liquid. Turn the dish over on a serving plate and decorate it with *foie gras* sliced into little scallops. Serve with a thick truffle sauce.

Sorbets au vin de Champagne

½ pint of water ~ 1 bottle of champagne ~ 6 oz sugar
1 lemon, squeezed ~ 4 oranges, squeezed
zest of a lemon ~ zest of the oranges

First make a sugar syrup by heating the sugar in the water in a saucepan until all the sugar is dissolved. Set aside to cool and then mix the juices of the lemon and oranges in a *sorbetier* with half the bottle of champagne, stirring constantly. Add the zest little by little and place the *sorbetier* in the refrigerator at the coldest setting. When the ices are set, gradually add the rest of the champagne.

Jambon à la Passy, pour relève

½ lb Parma ham ~ 2 egg yolks ~ ½ cup Madeira
¼ lb spinach leaves

Roll up the thinly sliced pieces of Parma ham into neat rolls. Put the egg yolks in an enamel saucepan and whisk them until they start to thicken. Put the saucepan in a simmering *bain-marie* and add the Madeira drop by drop, while still whisking. After all the Madeira has been added to the sauce, keep whisking until the sauce is really thick.

Arrange washed and dried spinach leaves on a serving platter and lay the Parma ham rolls neatly in a crown pattern on top. Pour the thick Madeira sauce over the ham rolls.

Côtelettes d'agneau à la dame d'Auteuil, aux pointes d'asperge

6 lamb chops ~ ½ lb of white asparagus heads
6 oz butter ~ 2 teaspoons salt ~ 2 teaspoons ground pepper
¼ cup chopped mint leaves

Rub the lamb chops with salt and pepper and sauté them quickly in butter at high temperature on both sides until they are dark brown. Arrange the white asparagus standing straight up in a asparagus steamer. Fill the steamer with 2 inches of water and steam the asparagus until the heads are just cooked. Take the asparagus out of the steamer and cut off the heads with some of the stems. Place the lamb chops on a serving platter and arrange the asparagus heads around the chops. Pour a thick butter sauce over the asparagus and sprinkle the chopped mint leaves over the lamb chops.

Macédoine de légumes

½ lb Belgian endive leaves ~ ½ lb *haricots verts* (or string beans)
1 red bell pepper ~ 1 yellow bell pepper ~ 3 small leeks ~ 2 eggs
½ cup *court-bouillon* (see above) ~ 4 tablespoons lemon juice
4 tablespoons butter ~ 2 tablespoons olive oil ~ 2 teaspoons crushed garlic
1 teaspoon salt ~ 1 teaspoon pepper ~ 1 teaspoon nutmeg

Wash the Belgian endives and pat dry with a cloth. Blanch the *haricots verts* in a little salted water with the lemon juice. Drain and dry them. Roast the red and yellow bell peppers in a hot oven, until the skin is slightly blackened. Peel the peppers and slice them *en julienne*. Cut the leeks lengthways and trim them into 1½-inch pieces and fry them in olive oil and butter. Add the crushed garlic to the leeks and sauté till the garlic is crisp, but not burnt. Pour in some *court-bouillon* and reduce. Arrange the Belgian endives at the bottom of a large shallow bowl and sprinkle the leeks on top of the endives;

followed by the *haricots verts* and the red and yellow bell peppers. Beat the two eggs in a small glass bowl and melt some butter in a skillet and pour in the beaten eggs. Cook slowly on a low heat, while stirring, until the eggs just start to stiffen. Take immediately off the heat and pour over the vegetables. Dust the eggs with some nutmeg.

Meringues du roi

2 egg whites ~ 4 oz caster sugar
4 oz finely chopped unsalted pistachio nuts ~ ¼ pint heavy cream
¼ cup lemon rind

Line a baking tray with greaseproof paper. Whisk the egg whites until very stiff. Beat in half the sugar and whisk until stiff again, then fold in the chopped pistachio and the remaining sugar. Spoon the meringue into a piping bag with a large nozzle and pipe little blobs on the prepared baking tray. Bake in the oven at 250°F (gas mark 1/2), for 2 hours until the meringues are firm and still white. Take the meringues off the tray and leave to cool. Whip the heavy cream until stiff and whisk in the lemon rinds. Spoon the whipped cream into a glass serving bowl and top it with the pistachio *meringues du roi*.

"To lengthen thy Life, lessen thy Meals"   BENJAMIN FRANKLIN

Thanksgiving Turkey

THANKSGIVING SALAD

~

ROAST TURKEY

~

CRANBERRY SAUCE

~

THANKSGIVING YAMS

~

SUCCOTASH

~

PUMPKIN PIE

When the Pilgrims sailed across the Atlantic on the Mayflower and landed at the rocky shores at Plymouth, they were met by the Wampanoags Indians, who belonged to the Algonquin-speaking people. The Wampanoags were a nomadic tribe moving several times during the year to get food. They fished the rivers in the springtime to catch salmon and in the hunting season they would move to the forests to hunt deer. During the winter they lived off the food they had planted and hunted in earlier months. The Pilgrims did not get off to an easy start; the wheat they had brought with them from England to plant in their new territory would not grow in the rocky soil. Many of them died of starvation and they needed to learn new ways to survive in their new world. The Wampanoags taught the Pilgrims how to grow corn and cultivate other vegetables, and how to hunt deer and dig for clams. They explained which plants were poisonous and which could be used as medicine, how to tap the sap from the maple tree and how to use fish as fertilizer. Gradually life was becoming better for the Pilgrims: the corn they had planted was growing well and there was enough stored food for the winter. They were in good health now; they knew more about surviving in their new land. The Pilgrims decided to share a thanksgiving feast in November with the Indians.

The Wampanoags, like all the Algonquin tribes, held six thanksgivings a year. At the beginning of the Algonquin calendar they held the Maple Dance, to give thanks to the Creator for giving them the maple tree and its syrup. The second thanksgiving was a planting feast, where all the seeds were blessed for a good harvest, and when the first fruits came into season the third thanksgiving was celebrated. In the summer, there was a thanksgiving for the corn and in the autumn came the fifth one in celebration of the harvest and all the food that the good earth had yielded. The sixth and last thanksgiving was in mid-winter to commemorate the passing of the old year.

For the thanksgiving feast with the Pilgrims the Wampanoags brought wild turkeys, venison, corn, squash, beans, fish, bread and berries to the table. The Pilgrim wives all stood quietly behind the tables, waiting for their men to finish eating, before they were allowed to eat, for that was their custom. The first Pilgrim thanksgiving with turkey and all the other fruits of the earth was the Indians' fifth thanksgiving of the year.

In later years Benjamin Franklin showed much sympathy for the turkey and explained why the turkey should have been selected as the American national symbol.

"I wish the Bald Eagle had not been chosen as the Representative of this Country; he is a bird of bad moral Character; he does not get his Living honestly. The humble Turkey minds his own Business, respecting the Rights of others. The Turkey is a unique American Creature."

Thanksgiving Salad

4 cups cranberries ~ 2 oranges, cut into big pieces
2 cups celery, sliced ~ 2 cups sugar ~ 6 oz gelatine
1 cup whipped cream ~ 1 cup mayonnaise ~ 2 teaspoons salt

Dissolve gelatine in boiling water and refrigerate until set. Peel the oranges and remove the white membranes. Put the cranberries and the peeled oranges in a food processor with the sugar, celery and salt. Blend the mixture and fold into the slightly thickened gelatine. Slightly oil a glass bowl and put the mixture into it. Set back in the refrigerator to chill. Serve with a mixture of whipped cream and mayonnaise.

Roast Turkey

10–12 lb turkey ~ sage stuffing or stuffing of your choice
4 tablespoons cranberry jelly ~ 1 cup lemon juice

Roast the turkey in 375°F (gas mark 5) oven for 2½ hours, while basting regularly. Mix cranberry jelly and lemon juice. Add hot water drop by drop and mix to a smooth paste. Brush the turkey with the cranberry paste every 15 to 20 minutes. The turkey should be cooked after 3½–4 hours.

Benjamin Franklin's Turkey Stuffing

2 cups of breadcrumbs ~ 6 skinned pork sausages
1 cup of chopped mushrooms ~ ½ cup raisins
1 apple ~ 1 large chopped sweet onion ~ 2 crushed cloves of garlic
1 tablespoon of fresh sage ~ 1 tablespoon of sweet herbs
4 fillets of anchovy ~ 2 tablespoons of butter ~ 2 tablespoons of Calvados
1 beaten egg ~ 2 tablespoons of chopped parsley
1 teaspoon of salt ~ 1 teaspoon of ground black pepper

Melt the butter in a frying pan and sauté the chopped onions together with the crushed garlic until they turn light brown. Add the chopped mushrooms and sauté until they have just softened. Peel and core the apple and cut it into approximately ½ inch cubes. Grind the fillets of anchovy into a paste, using a pestle and mortar. Break with a fork the skinned pork sausages into small pieces. Combine the sausage pieces with all other ingredients into a homogeneous stuffing, ready to fill the turkey's neck and body cavity. Sew up the bird and truss its legs.

Benjamin Franklin's Turkey Gravy

turkey giblets (liver, heart and gizzard) ~ 1 small sweet onion
2 cloves ~ 2 bay leaves ~ 1 bundle of sweet herbs ~ 1 tablespoon cornflour
1 cup red wine ~ 1 teaspoon salt ~ 1 teaspoon ground black pepper

To make a stock, place the giblets with the onion, cloves, bay leaves and sweet herbs in a saucepan of water and add the pepper and salt. Cover the pan and let it simmer for 1 hour and strain afterwards.

To make the gravy, stir the cornflour into the turkey drippings in the roasting pan to make a homogeneous paste. Add then gradually the cup of red wine, and the giblet stock while stirring continuously, and bring it to a simmer until the gravy starts to thicken.

Cranberry Sauce

12 oz cranberries ~ 1 cup sugar ~ 1 teaspoon ground cinnamon
1 cup water

Combine the cranberries, sugar and water in a saucepan. Bring to the boil. Simmer for about 10 minutes until thickened. Blend in cinnamon and set aside to cool.

Thanksgiving Yams

2 lbs yams ~ ½ cup butter ~ 4 tablespoons lemon juice ~ 8 oz dried apricots
4 oz pecans ~ ¼ cup brown sugar ~ 1 teaspoon ground ginger
2 teaspoons ground cinnamon ~ ½ teaspoon ground cloves
1 teaspoon salt ~ 1 teaspoon pepper

Boil the yams in salted water until cooked. Drain them, pat dry and slice them. Cook the apricots in water until soft and reduce the liquid. Add butter, brown sugar, lemon juice, ginger, cinnamon, cloves and stir until the sugar is dissolved.

Arrange the sliced yams in a buttered baking dish and sprinkle with salt and pepper. Pour the cooked apricots over the yams and top with the pecans. Bake in a preheated 375°F (gas mark 5) oven for 30–35 minutes.

Succotash

2 cups fresh and cooked corn kernels ~ 1 cup lima beans ~ ½ cup peas
1 cup diced salt pork ~ 1 tablespoon butter ~ 1 tablespoon crushed garlic
2 teaspoons brown sugar ~ 1 teaspoon salt ~ 1 teaspoon black pepper

Sauté the diced salt pork with the crushed garlic in the butter till light brown. Stir in the brown sugar, salt and pepper. Add the corn kernels, lima beans and peas. Keep stirring over medium heat until hot.

*"Plough deep, while Sluggards sleep; And you shall have Corn,
to sell and to keep"*   BENJAMIN FRANKLIN

Pumpkin Pie

1½ cups cooked pumpkin ~ 1 cup sliced bananas
1½ cups evaporated milk ~ 2 eggs, beaten ~ 1 cup brown sugar
2 tablespoons molasses ~ ½ teaspoon salt
2 teaspoons ground cinnamon ~ 1 teaspoon ground ginger
¼ teaspoon ground cloves

Mix all ingredients together in a glass bowl and place them in an unbaked 9-inch piecrust.

Bake at 450°F (gas mark 8) for 10 minutes and then reduce to 350°F (gas mark 4) for 20 minutes, until an inserted knife comes out clean. Take the pie out and decorate it with the banana slices and bake for 10 minutes more. Serve with whipped cream.

THE PENNSYLVANIA GAZETTE, 1746

"In Pursuance of the Governor's late Proclamation for that Purpose, Thursday last was observed here with a becoming Solemnity, as a Day of Publick Thanksgiving to Almighty God, for the Suppression of the Rebellion in Scotland, &c. Great Numbers of People attended at all the Places of Worship in the fore Part of the Day; and his Honour the Governor entertained near a hundred of the principal Gentlemen and Inhabitants of the City at Dinner; where our Happiness under the present Constitution, both in Church and State, and the great Obligations we have to the Family on the Throne, were properly and decently remember'd."

Receipt for making Sweet Corn, and Suckahtash
by Benjamin Franklin

Take the Ears of Indian Corn when in the Milk, and boil them almost enough to eat, then shell it, and spread it on a Cloth very thin, and dry it in the Sun till it shrinks to half its Bigness, and becomes very hard, then put it into any dry Cask, and it will keep the Year round. When you use it, you must put it into a Pot, and let it warm moderately over a Fire for three or four Hours, but which Means it swells considerably, then boil it till you find 'tis fit to eat. In order to make Suckahtash, 'tis only putting about a third Part of Beans with the Corn when you boil it.

Thanksgiving Prayer

At the age of 22 Benjamin Franklin composed a Thanksgiving prayer to be used at the end of the harvest.

> For Peace and Liberty, for Good and
> Raiment, for Corn and Wine and Milk
> and every other Nourishment
> Good God I thank Thee
>
> For the common Benefits of Air and
> Light, for useful Fire and delicious Water
> Good God I thank Thee
>
> For Knowledge and Literature and
> every useful Art, for my Friends, and their
> Prosperity and for the Fewness of my Enemies
> Good God I thank Thee
>
> For all the innumerable Benefits,
> for Life, for Reason, for Health,
> for Joy and every pleasant Hour
> Good God I thank Thee

Craven Street Craving

GREEN PEA SOUP

~

VENISON MEAT LOAF

~

BISCUITS AND PICKL'D CUCUMBERS

~

NEWTON PIPPIN UPSIDE-DOWN

CRAVEN STREET GAZETTE. No 113.
Saturday, Sept. 22, 1770

> "We hear that the *great* Person (so called for his enormous Size) of a certain Family in a certain Street, is grievously affected at the late Changes, and could hardly be comforted this Morning, tho' the new Ministry promised him a roasted Shoulder of Mutton, and Potatoes, for his Dinner."

〰️〰️〰️

INSTRUCTIONS TO BENJAMIN FRANKLIN Esqr. One of the Commissioners appointed by the Assembly of the Province of Pennsylvania to obtain Redress of those several Infractions of the Royal Grant and Proprietary Charter, and other Aggrievances, which the People of this Province very justly complain of. In Assembly March 31st. 1757.

> You are to proceed immediately to Great Britain in the first Packet Boat that sails from New York, or by the next convenient Opportunity after your Receipt of these Instructions.
>
> If you shou'd be taken by the Enemy, you advise the House by the first opportunity with your ... [*remainder missing*]

Benjamin Franklin arrived in London in 1757 as an Agent of the Pennsylvania Assembly. His mission was to lobby the Crown and Parliament about grievances the Assembly had towards the Penn family, owners of the Proprietary Province of Pennsylvania. The main grievance of the people of Pennsylvania against the Penn family was that, being the Proprietors of the Province, all their lands were untaxed, while the other citizens of Pennsylvania had to pay taxes on their properties. Franklin also met one of the proprietors, Thomas Penn, in London, to discuss what was on Pennsylvania's liver. The meeting was a disaster for Franklin; he was snubbed by Penn in a very humiliating way. It was obvious, the Penns did not want to hear from an agent of the Assembly that they should pay their fair share in taxes. By their father William Penn, the family had extracted certain rights from the Crown, which by their reckoning were etched in stone. The Penns were not to give up on their rightful privileges, whether Franklin came to town or not. Later Franklin spoke of Penn: "When I meet him anywhere, there appears in his wretched countenance a strange mixture of hatred, anger, fear and vexation. I hope that the Penns would be gibbeted up as they deserve, to rot and stink in the nostrils of posterity."

Many years later Franklin had booked a victory, albeit a small one; he had managed to have the estates of the Penn family subjected to taxation. It was agreed that only those lands of the Penns in Pennsylvania that had been surveyed would be taxed, whereas their vast unsurveyed lands would remain tax-exempt. Later on during the 1760s Benjamin Franklin would also assume agency of Massachusetts, New Jersey, and Georgia.

When Benjamin Franklin came to London in 1757 he rented a few rooms in the house of Margaret Stevenson, a widow who was living on Craven Street with her daughter Mary, also known as Polly. There he paid Margaret 11s. 5d. for dinner on the night he presumably moved in. He lived in this house with his son William, who was going to read law at Middle Temple and with his black servant Peter. Benjamin later wrote to his wife Deborah in Philadelphia:

> "As you desire to know several Particulars about me, I now let you know that I lodge in Craven Street near Charing Cross, Westminster; We have four Rooms

furnished, and every thing about us pretty genteel, but Living here is in every respect very expensive. Billy is with me, and very serviceable. Peter has behav'd very well. Goodeys I now and then get a few; but roasting Apples seldom, I wish you had sent me some; and I wonder how you, that us'd to think of every thing, came to forget it. Newton Pippins would have been the most acceptable".

ᘓᘔ ᘓᘔᘓ ᘓᘔ

THE CRAVEN STREET GAZETTE. No 113.
Saturday, Sept.22, 1770

"We hear that the Lady Chamberlain of the Household went to Market this Morning by her own self, gave the Butcher whatever he ask'd for the Mutton, and had no Dispute with the Potatoe Woman — to their great Amazement — at the Change of Times!"

The house was to be his home in London from 1757 to 1762 and from 1764 to 1775. Margaret Stevenson became an influence on the provincial Benjamin Franklin. She took good care of him; she was an excellent cook, and looked after his linen and aired his shirts. It was in Craven Street that he started taking his summer "air baths"; where he would sit in his "birthday suit", reading a book, while letting his skin soak up the fresh air. Benjamin Franklin also developed here a good taste for the finer things in life, as he wrote to Deborah in 1758:

"I send you by Capt. Budden, a large Case mark'd D. F. No. 1. and a small Box D. F. No. 2. In the large Case is another small Box, containing some English China; viz. Melons and Leaves for a Dessert Fruit and Cream, or the like, a Bowl remarkable for the Neatness of the Figures, made at Bow, near this City; some Coffee Cups of the same; a Worcester Bowl, ordinary. To show the Difference of Workmanship there is something from all the China Works in England; and one old true China Basin mended, of an odd Colour. The same Box contains 4 Silver Salt Ladles, newest, but ugliest, Fashion; a little Instrument to Core Apples; another to make little Turnips out of great ones; Six coarse diaper Breakfast Cloths; they are to spread on the Tea Table, for no body breakfasts here on the naked Table, but on the Cloth set a large Tea Board with the Cups; there is also a little Basket, a Present from Mrs Stevenson to Sally, and a Pair of Garters for you which were knit by the young Lady her Daughter, who favour'd me with a Pair of the same kind, the only ones I have been able to wear; as they need not be bound tight, the Ridges in them preventing their Slipping. We send them therefore as a Curiosity for the Form, more than for the Value. Goody Smith may, if she pleases, make such for me hereafter, and they will suit her own fat Knees. My Love to her.

In the great Case, besides the little Box, is contain'd some Carpeting for the best Room Floor. There is enough for one large or two small ones; it is to be sow'd together, the Edges being first fell'd down, and Care taken to

[69]

make the Figures meet exactly: there is Bordering for the same. This was my Fancy.

Also two large fine Flanders Bed Ticks, and two pair large superfine Blankets, 2 fine Damask Table Cloths and Napkins, and 43 Ells of Ghentish Sheeting Holland; these you ordered. There is also 56 Yards of Cotton printed curiously from Copper Plates, a new Invention, to make Bed and Window Curtains; and 7 Yards Chair Bottoms printed in the same Way, very neat; these were my Fancy; but Mrs Stevenson tells me I did wrong not to buy both of the same Colour.

Also 7 Yards of printed Cotton, blue Ground, to make you a Gown; I bought it by Candlelight, and lik'd it then, but not so well afterwards: if you do not fancy it, send it as a Present from me to Sister Jenny. There is a better Gown for you of flower'd Tissue, 16 Yards, of Mrs Stevenson's Fancy, cost 9 Guineas; and I think it a great Beauty; there was no more of the Sort, or you should have had enough for a Negligee or Suit.

There is also a Snuffers, Snuff Stand and Extinguisher, of Steel, which I sent for the Beauty of the Work; the Extinguisher is for Sperma Ceti Candles only, and is of a new Contrivance to preserve the Snuff upon the Candle. There is also some Musick Billy bought for his Sister, and some Pamphlets for the Speaker and for Susy Wright. A Mahogany and a little Shagrin Box with Microscopes and other Optical Instruments loose, are for Mr Allison if he likes them; if not, put them in my Room 'till I return. I send the Invoice of them, and wrote to him formerly the Reason of my exceeding his Orders. There are also two Sets of Books a Present from me to Sally, *the World* and *the Connoisseur*; my Love to her.

I forgot to mention another of my Fancyings, viz. a Pair of Silk Blankets, very fine. They are of a new kind, were just taken in a French Prize, and such were never seen in England before: they are called Blankets; but I think will be very neat to cover a Summer Bed instead of a Quilt or Counterpane. I had no Choice, so you will excuse the Soil on some of the Folds; your Neighbour Forster can get it off. I also forgot, among the China, to mention a large fine Jugg for Beer, to stand in the Cooler. I fell in Love with it at first Sight; for I thought it look'd like a fat jolly Dame, clean and tidy, with a neat blue and white Calico Gown on, good natur'd and lovely, and put me in mind of — Somebody. It has the Coffee Cups in its Belly, pack'd in best Crystal Salt, of a peculiar nice Flavour, for the Table, not to be powder'd. No.2 contains cut Table Glass of several Sorts. I am about buying a compleat Set of Table China, 2 Cases of silver handled Knives and Forks, and 2 pair Silver Candlesticks; but these shall keep to use here till my Return, as I am obliged sometimes to entertain polite Company."

<hr />

THE CRAVEN STREET GAZETTE. No 113.
Saturday, Sept.22, 1770

"We have good Authority to assure our Readers, that a Cabinet Council was held this Afternoon at Tea; the Subject of which was a Proposal for the

Reformation of Manners, and a more strict Observation of the Lord's Day. The Result was, an unanimous Resolution that no Meat should be dress'd tomorrow; whereby the Cook and the first Minister will both be at Liberty to go to Church, the one having nothing to do, and the other no Roast to rule. It seems the cold Shoulder of Mutton, and the Applepye, were thought sufficient for Sunday's Dinner. All pious People applaud this Measure, and 'tis thought the new Ministry will soon become popular."

In return Deborah sent him and Margaret Stevenson all kinds of local products from the Colonies, like dried venison, bacon, green peas, cranberries, smoked hams. And Newton Pippins, as he had asked for:

"I shall only acknowledge the Receipt of the Apples; those in the Boxes turn'd out much better than those in the Barrels; and amongst the Boxes, Billy's rather the best." Benjamin thanked Deborah by saying: "The dried Venison was very acceptable, and I thank you for it. We have had it constantly shav'd to eat with our Bread and Butter for Breakfast, and this Week saw the last of it. The Bacon still holds out; for we are choice of it. Some Rashers of it yesterday relish'd a Dish of Green Pease. Mrs Stevenson thinks there never was any in England so good. The smok'd Beef was also excellent."

꧁ ꧂ ꧁

THE CRAVEN STREET GAZETTE. No 113.
Sunday, Sept. 23

"Notwithstanding yesterday's solemn Order of Council, no body went to Church to day. It seems the *great* Person's broad-built-bulk lay so long abed, that Breakfast was not over 'till it was too late to dress. At least this is the Excuse. In fine, it seems a vain thing to hope Reformation from the Example of our great Folks. The Cook and the Minister, however, both took Advantage of the Order so far, as to save themselves all Trouble, and the Clause of *cold Dinner* was enforc'd, tho' the *going to Church* was dispens'd with."

Green Pea Soup

"Take a small Knuckle of Veal, about three or four Pounds, chop it all to Pieces, and set it on the Fire in six Quarts of Water. Put to it a little Piece of lean Bacon, about half an Ounce, steeped in Vinegar an Hour, four or five Blades of Mace, three or four Cloves, twelve Pepper-corns of Black Pepper, twelve of White, a little Bundle of Sweet Herbs and Parsley and a little Piece of Upper Crust toasted crisp. Cover it close, and let it boil softly over a slow Fire till Half is wasted. Then strain it off, and put to it a Pint of Green Peas and a Lettuce cut small, four Heads of Sellery cut very small, and washed clean. Cover it close, and let it stew very softly over a slow Fire two Hours. In the mean Time boil a Pint of old Peas in a Pint of Water very tender, and strain them well through a coarse Hair-sieve and all the Pulp, then pour it into the Soop, and let it boil together. Season with Salt to your Palate, but not too much. Fry a French Roll crisp, put it into your Dish, and pour your Soop in. Be sure there be full two Quarts. Mutton Gravy will do, if you have no Veal. Or a Shin of Beef chopped to Pieces. A few Asparagus-Tops are very good in it."

THE CRAVEN STREET GAZETTE. No 113.
Monday, Sept. 24.

"We are credibly informed, that the great Person dined this Day with the Club at the Cat-and-Bagpipes (John Ellicot's Monday Club at The George and Vulture) in the City, on cold Round of boil'd Beef. This, it seems, he was under some Necessity of Doing (tho' he rather dislikes Beef) because truly the Ministers were to be all abroad somewhere to dine on hot roast Venison."

Venison Meat Loaf

2 lbs ground venison ~ ½ cup chopped bacon ~ 2 eggs ~ 1 cup bread crumbs
1 sweet onion, finely chopped ~ 1 cup chopped mushrooms
4 tablespoons port ~ ½ cup chopped parsley
1 teaspoon salt ~ 1 teaspoon pepper

Fry chopped bacon in a skillet till crisp. Add onions, mushrooms and parsley and cook till it becomes a semi-dry mixture. In a glass bowl combine the ground venison with the mixture. Add slightly beaten eggs, bread-crumbs and port. Mix well with the hands and season with pepper and salt. Put new mixture in a buttered loaf dish and bake in a 350°F (gas mark 4) oven for 1½ hours.

THE CRAVEN STREET GAZETTE. No 113.
Monday, Sept. 24.

"It is currently reported, that poor Nanny had nothing for Dinner in the Kitchen, for herself and Puss, but the Scrapings of the Bones of Saturday's Mutton."

Biscuits and Pickl'd Cucumbers

"Take the large Cucumbers before they are too ripe. Slice them the thickness of Crown-piece in a Pewter Dish. To every Dozen of Cucumbers slice two large Onions thin, and so on till you have filled your Dish, with a Handful of Salt between every Row. Then cover them with another Pewter Dish, and let them stand twenty-four Hours, then put them in a Cullender, and let them drain very well. Put them into a Jar, and with them a little Dill and Fennel in a small Quantity. Cover them over with White Wine Vinegar, and let them stand four Hours. Pour the Vinegar from them into a Copper Sauce-pan, and boil it with a little Salt. Put to the Cucumbers a little Mace, a little whole Pepper, a large Race of Ginger sliced, and then pour the boiling Vinegar on. Cover them close, and when they are cold, tie them down. They will be fit to eat in two or three Days."

A side dish of biscuits and pickles was common practice in the 18th century, when biscuits and pickles stayed on the table throughout the meal.

"Squeamish stomachs cannot eat without pickles"

BENJAMIN FRANKLIN

THE CRAVEN STREET GAZETTE. No 113.

Tuesday, Sept. 25.

"The Publick may be assured, that this Morning a certain *great Person* was ask'd very complaisantly by the Mistress of the Household, if he would chuse to have the Blade Bone of Saturday's Mutton that had been kept for his Dinner to Day, *broil'd* or *cold?* He answer'd gravely, *If there is any Flesh on it, it may be broil'd; if not, it may as well be cold.* Orders were accordingly given for broiling it. But when it came to Table, there was indeed so very little Flesh, or rather none at all. Puss having din'd on it yesterday after Nanny."

Newton Pippin Upside-Down

1 lb Pippin apples, peeled, cored and sliced ~ ¾ cup sugar
½ lb unsalted butter ~ 1 egg ~ 1¼ cups flour ~ 2 teaspoons baking powder
½ teaspoon salt ~ 1 cup milk

Butter the bottom of a 9-inch diameter, 1½-inch deep baking pan with 2 oz of soft, unsalted butter. Sprinkle ½ cup of sugar evenly over the bottom and spread the slices of apple evenly out on top.

[73]

Mix together the remaining 6 oz of softened sweet butter with ½ cup of sugar. Add the egg and beat till combined. In another bowl, sieve the flour, baking powder and salt together. Stir flour mix into the batter, bit by bit, alternate with drops of milk. Stir the batter until combined and pour over the apples and smooth the top. Preheat oven at 350°F (gas mark 4) and bake for 1 hour, till lightly browned. Transfer to a rack and let cool for a while. Turn cake over onto a platter and eat warm.

> *"An apple a day, keeps the doctor away"*   BENJAMIN FRANKLIN

To the Publisher of the Craven Street Gazette

Sir,

I make no doubt of the Truth of what the Papers tell us, that a certain great *Person* has been half-starved on the bare Blade-bone, *of a Sheep* (I cannot call it *of Mutton* because none was on it) by a Set of the most careless, thoughtless, inconsiderate, corrupt, ignorant, blundering, foolish, crafty, and Knavish Ministers, that ever got into a House and pretended to govern a Family and provide a Dinner. Alas, for the poor Old England of Craven Street! If these nefarious Wretches continue in Power another Week, the Nation will be ruined — Undone! — totally undone, if the Queen does not return; or (which is better) turn them all out and appoint me and my Friends to succeed them. I am a great Admirer of your useful and impartial Paper; and therefore request you will insert this without fail; from Your humble Servant INDIGNATION.

[APPLES]

Throughout the ages a whole gamut of fruits have been called apples: the avocado, the aubergine, the date, the lemon and the orange, the pomegranate, the peach and the melon, the pineapple and the tomato. Apples (*pyrus malus*) were first recorded in the 13th century BC in ancient Egypt, when Ramesses II ordered apple trees to be planted in the Nile delta. The ancient Greeks were cultivating apples in the 7th century BC. Apples were rare and expensive then. Solon, the Athenian statesman, signed a decree stating that married couples could only ever consume one apple between them, before going to bed on their wedding night. The Romans grew different varieties of apples which were generally bought to be eaten raw, but in some ancient Roman recipes, apples are mentioned in dishes like roast pork.

In medieval England apples were available to the populace at large and were sold by street vendors. Later in the 17th century apples and other raw fruit became associated with disease. Subsequently they were used in well-cooked tarts and pies. Early American settlers also baked their apples in pies, to preserve them on their long journeys through the new territories. Hence the expression: "as American as apple pie". John Chapman, popularly known as Johnny Appleseed, wandered the states of Ohio, Indiana and Pennsylvania randomly sowing apples pips.

〰〰〰

To the Publisher of the Craven Street Gazette

Sir,

Your Correspondent *Indignation* has made a fine Story in your Paper against our Cravenstreet Ministry, as if they meant to starve his Highness, giving him only a bare Blade Bone for his Dinner, while they riot upon roast Venison, &c. The Wickedness of Writers in this Age is truly amazing! I believe we never had since the Foundation of our State, a more faithful, upright, worthy, careful, considerate, incorrupt, discreet, wise, prudent and beneficent Ministry than the present. But if even the Angel Gabriel would condescend to be our Minister and provide our Dinners, he could scarcely escape Newspaper defamation from a Gang of hungry ever-restless, discontented and malicious Scribblers. It is, Sir, a piece of Justice you owe our righteous Administration to undeceive the Publick on this [Occasion], by assuring them [of] the Fact, which is, that there was provided, and actually smoking on the table under his Royal Nose at the same Instant, as fine a Piece of Ribbs of Beef, roasted, as ever Knife was put into; with Potatoes, Horse radish, pickled Walnuts, &c. which Beef his Highness might have eaten of, if so he had pleased to do; and which he forbore to do, merely from whimsical Opinion (with Respect be it spoken) that Beef doth not with him perspire well, but makes his Back itch, to his no small Vexation, now that he hath lost the little Chinese Ivory Hand [at] the End of a Stick, commonly called a Scratchback, presented to him by her Majesty. This is the Truth; and if your boasted Impartiality is real, you will not hesitate a Moment to insert this Letter in your very next Paper. I am, tho' a little angry with you at present. Yours as you behave

A HATER OF SCANDAL.

THE CRAVEN STREET GAZETTE. No 113.

Postscript. Wednesday, Sept. 26.

"Those in the Secret of Affairs do not scruple to assert soundly, that our present First Ministress is very notable, having this Day been to Market, bought excellent Mutton Chops, and Apples 4 a penny, made a very fine Applepye with her own Hands, and mended two pair of Breeches."

Marriages: None since our last; but Puss begins to go a Courting.

Deaths: In the back Closet, and elsewhere, many poor Mice.

Stocks: Biscuits very low

Buckwheat and Indian meal, both sour.

Tea, lowering daily in the Canister.

Galley Gourmet

DRESSED COD'S HEAD

~

DOLPHIN DELIGHT

~

PICKL'D MUSHROOM FOR THE SEA

~

WHIPPING POST PUDDING

~

BERKSHIRE RUM PUNCH

Benjamin Franklin's first visit to London lasted eighteen months. After that he saw no means to improve his fortune and set sail back to Philadelphia. On 23 July, 1726 he sailed from Gravesend on the *Berkshire*. It took the *Berkshire* almost three months to reach Philadelphia, much longer than the 30 days it would take Franklin to sail from New York to Falmouth with his son William in 1757. Since 1745 Franklin had been wondering why ships sailing from the colonies to England had a quicker voyage than those returning. He asked various ships' captains about the time difference between the voyages out and back. A kind of sea current was often mentioned. Later, in 1767 he wrote that a voyager would know when he was in the Gulf Stream by the warmth of the water.

Friday, 22 July, 1726

"Yesterday in the Afternoon we left London, and came to an Anchor off Gravesend. This Gravesend is a cursed biting Place; the chief Dependence of the People being the Advantage of them, and give half what you ask, you pay twice as much as the Thing is worth. Thank God, we shall leave tomorrow...."

Sunday, 24 July, 1726

"This Morning we weigh'd Anchor, and coming to the Downs, we set our Pilot ashore at Deal, and pass'd through. On the left Hand appears the Coast of France at a Distance, and on the Right is the Town and Castle of Dover, with the green Hills and chalky Cliffs of England, to which we must now bid farewell. Albion, farewell! ..."

Sunday, July 31, 1726

"This Morning the Wind being moderate, our Pilot design'd to weigh, and taking Advantage of the Tide, get a little further to windward. Upon which the Boat came ashore, to hasten us on board. We had sooner return'd and hoist'd in our Boat but the Wind began again to blow very hard at West, insomuch that instead of going any further, we were oblig'd to weigh and run down again to Cowes for the Sake of more secure Riding, where we came to an Anchor again in a very little time; and the Pudding which our Mess made and put into the Pot at Yarmouth we dined upon at Cowes".

Saturday, August 27, 1726

"Clear'd up this Morning, and the Wind settl'd westerly. Two Dolphins follow'd us this Afternoon: we hook'd one and struck the other with the Fizgig; but they both escap'd us, and we saw them no more".

Monday, August 29, 1726

"Wind still hard West. Two Dolphins follow'd us this Day; we struck them, but they both escap'd".

Friday, September 2, 1726

This Morning the Wind changed; a little fair. We caught a couple of Dolphins, and fried them for Dinner. They eat indifferent well. These Fish make a glorious Appearance in the Water; their Bodies are of bright green, mixed with a silver Colour, and their Tails of a shining golden yellow; but all this vanishes presently after they are taken out of their Element, and they change all over to a light grey. I observed that cutting off Pieces of a just-caught, living Dolphin for Baits, those Pieces did not lose their lustre and fine Colours when the Dolphin died, but retained perfectly. Every one takes notice of that vulgar error of the Painters, who always represent this Fish monstrously crooked and deformed, when it is in reality as beautiful and well shaped a Fish as any that swims. I cannot think what should be the original of the Chimera of theirs, (since there is not a Creature in nature that in the least resembles their Dolphin) unless it proceeded at first from a false Imitation of a Fish in the Posture of leaping, which they have since improved into a crooked monster with a Head and Eyes like a Bull, a Hogs Snout, and a Tail like a blown Tulip. But the Sailors give me another Reason, though a wimsical one, viz. that as this most beautiful Fish is only to be caught at Sea, and that very far to the Southward, they say the Painters wilfully deform it in their Representations, lest pregnant women should long for what it is impossible to procure for them.

Friday, September 9, 1726

"This afternoon we took four large Dolphins, three with a Hook and Line, and the fourth we struck with a Fizgig. The Bait was a Candle with two Feathers stuck in it, one on each Side, in Imitation of a Flying-fish, which are the common Prey of the Dolphins. They appeared extremely eager and hungry, and snapped up the Hook as soon as it ever touched the Water. When we came to open them, we found in the Belly of one, a small Dolphin half digested. Certainly they were half famished, or are naturally very savage to devour those of their own Species".

Saturday, September 10, 1726

"This day we dined upon the dolphins we caught yesterday, three of them sufficing the whole ship, being twenty-one persons".

Tuesday, September 20, 1726

"The Wind is now westerly again, to our great Mortification; and we are to an Allowance of Bread, two Biscuits and a Half a Day".

Wednesday, September 21, 1726

"This Morning our Steward was brought to the Geers and whipp'd, for making an extravagant use of Flour in the Puddings, and for several other Misdemeanors. It had been perfectly calm all this Day, and very hot. I was determin'd to wash myself in the Sea to-day, and should have done so had not the Appearance of a Shark, that mortal Enemy to Swimmers, deterr'd me: he seem'd to be about five Feet long, moves round the Ship at some Distance in a slow majestic Manner, attend'd by near a Dozen of those they call Pilot-fish, of different Sizes; the Largest of them is not so big as a small Mackerel, and the Smallest not bigger than my little Finger. A Shark is never seen without a Retinue of these, who are his Purveyors, discovering and distinguishing his Prey for him; while he in return gratefully protects them from the ravenous hungry Dolphin. They are commonly count'd a very greedy Fish; yet this refuses to meddle with the Bait we have thrown out for him. 'Tis likely he has lately made a full Meal".

Tuesday, September 27, 1726

"The fair Wind continues still. I have laid a Bowl of Punch that we are in Philadelphia next Saturday se'nnight, for we reckon ourselves not above 150 Leagues from Land. The Snow keeps us company still".

Monday, October 3, 1726

"The Water is now very visibly chang'd to the Eyes of all except the Captain and Mate, and they will by no means allow it; I suppose because they did not see it first. Abundance of Dolphins are about us, but they are very shy, and keep a Distance. Wind North West".

Tuesday Night, October 4, 1726

"Since Eleven o'Clock we have struck three fine Dolphins, which are a great refreshment to us. This Afternoon we have seen Abundance of Grampuses, which are seldom far from Land; but towards Evening we had a more evident Token, to wit, a little tired Bird, something like a Lark, came on board us, who certainly is an American, and 'tis likely was ashore this Day. It is now calm. We hope for a fair Wind next".

Thursday, October 6, 1726

"This Morning abundance of Grass, Rock-weed, &c. pass'd by us; evident Tokens that Land is not far off. We hook'd a Dolphin this Morning that made us a good Breakfast. A Sail pass'd by us about Twelve o'Clock, and nobody saw her till she was too far astern to be spoken with. 'Tis very near calm; we saw another Sail a-head this Afternoon; but Night coming on, we could not speak with her, though we very much desir'd it: she stood to the Northward, and it is possible might have informed us how far we are from Land".

Sunday, October 9, 1726

"We have had the Wind fair all the Morning; at Twelve o'Clock we sound'd, perceiving the Water visibly chang'd, and struck Ground at twenty-five Fathoms, to our universal Joy. After Dinner one of our Mess went aloft to look out, and presently pronounc'd the long-wish'd for Sound, Land! Land!"

Tuesday, October 11, 1726

"This Morning we weigh'd Anchor with a gentle Breeze, and pass'd by Newcastle, whence they hail'd us and bade us welcome. 'Tis extreme fine Weather. The Sun enlivens our stiff Limbs with his glorious Rays of Warmth and Brightness. The Sky looks gay, with here and there a silver Cloud. The fresh Breezes from the Woods refresh us, the immediate Prospect of Liberty after so long and irksome Confinement ravishes us. In short all Things conspire to make this the most joyful Day I ever knew. About Eight at Night, the Wind failing us, we cast Anchor at Redbank, six Miles from Philadelphia, and thought we must be oblig'd to lie on board that Night: but some young Philadelphians happening to be out upon their Pleasure in a Boat, they came on board, offer'd to take us up with them; we accept'd of their kind Proposal, and about Ten o'Clock land'd at Philadelphia, heartily congratulating each other upon our having happily complet'd so tedious and dangerous a Voyage. Thank God!"

Dressed Cod's Head

1 cod's head ~ 1 pint of cockles ~ ½ lb crab meat ~ ½ pint white wine
1 small bundle of sweet herbs ~ 2 onions, finely chopped
1 teaspoon mace ~ 1 teaspoon nutmeg ~ 2 tablespoons oyster sauce
5 tablespoons melted butter

Cut the cod's head so that many good pieces of the body stay with it. Boil in salted water. Put the cockles and crab meat in a small pot with the half a pint of white wine. Add the bundle of sweet herbs, chopped onions, mace, nutmeg and the oyster sauce. Boil these until the liquid is evaporated, take out the bundle of sweet herbs and then add the melted butter. Drain cod's head well and put it on a serving dish. Arrange the cockles and crabmeat over and around the head with the cod's liver and roe. Garnish with lemon wedges and sprigs of parsley.

"Dolphin" Delight

4 dolphin fish steaks (shark or swordfish can be substituted)
2 tablespoons garlic ~ 4 tablespoons olive oil
2 teaspoons chopped gingerroot ~ 1 teaspoon salt ~ 1 teaspoon pepper
4 teaspoons soy sauce ~ 3 tablespoons finely chopped spring onions

Marinate the steaks in a mixture of the olive oil, garlic, ginger root, salt and pepper and soy sauce for about 15 minutes. Preheat broiler at the highest setting and broil quickly the steaks on both sides until brown. Garnish with chopped spring onions.

Pickl'd Mushroom for the Sea

"Wash the Mushrooms clean with a Piece of Flannel in Salt and water. Put them into a Sauce-pan and throw a little Salt over them. Let them boil up three Times in their own Liquor, then throw them into a Sieve to drain, and spread them on a clean Cloth; let them lie till cold, then put them in wide-mouth'd Bottles. Put in with them a good deal of whole Mace, a little Nutmeg sliced, and a few Cloves. Boil the Sugar-Vinegar of your own making, with a good deal of whole Pepper, some Races of Ginger, and two or three Bay-Leaves. Let it boil a few Minutes, then strain it, when it is cold pour it on, and fill the Bottles with fried Mutton Fat. Cork them, tie a Bladder, and then a Leather over them. Keep it down close, and in as cool a Place as possible".

Whipping Post Pudding

Pastry:

8 oz flour ~ 1 teaspoon salt ~ 3 oz butter ~ 2 egg yolks

Filling:

8 oz honey ~ 6 oz raisins ~ 3 tablespoons dry white wine
4 tablespoons heavy cream ~ 1 teaspoon mace

Sift the flour and salt into a glass bowl and rub the butter into the flour until the mixture crumbles. Rub in the egg yolks and knead into a firm dough until smooth. Cover and chill in the refrigerator for 30 minutes. Then roll out the dough and line a 9-inch pie dish with it. Gently heat the honey, raisins, white wine and mace in a saucepan and thicken with the heavy cream. Fill the dough-lined pie dish with the filling and bake in a preheated 400 F (gas mark 6) oven for 30–35 minutes, or until the pastry is cooked. The honey and raisins give a lovely sweet taste. Serve with whipped cream.

"Tart Words make no Friends: a Spoonful of Honey will catch more flies than a Gallon of Vinegar"   BENJAMIN FRANKLIN

Berkshire Rum Punch

1/2 pint of dark rum ~ 2 pints of claret ~ 2 teaspoon nutmeg
4 tablespoon sugar ~ 4 tablespoon lemon juice

Dissolve the sugar in the rum. Add nutmeg and lemon juice. Stir thoroughly while pouring in the claret. Chill and serve with slices of lemon. In the colonies during the 1770s Americans were drinking an average of 3 imperial gallons of rum a year.

[HONEY]

Since the earliest days of recorded history, people have been using honey as a food, as a preservative and as medicine. Cave paintings from Neolithic times show people gathering honeycombs. Honey three thousand years old has been found in Egyptian pyramids, but it was dark and dry. The ancient Greeks and Romans used honey for embalming and preserving food.

[RUM]

The word rum either finds its origin in the word 'rumbullion' (great tumult), or else it was named after 'Ron Bacardi', the original distiller of white Cuban rum, with now the world's largest production of rum on the island of Puerto Rico. The first known use of the word rum dates back to 1654. Rum is made from the juices and molasses of the sugar cane. The harvested cane is brought to the sugar mills, where it is crushed through heavy rollers, to extract the juice. The juice is then boiled to reduce the water contents and to concentrate the sugar, until it turns into a thick syrup. The sugar in the syrup is subsequently separated and what remains are the molasses, which are then fermented and distilled. The end product is the rum, which is naturally colourless and only becomes dark when caramel is added. The legend of rum goes that the sugar cane was brought to the West Indies by Christopher Columbus from the Canary Islands, that in their turn had received the cane from the Orient. Rum has been known to be distilled by the Spanish in Hispaniola as early as the first decade of the 17th century. At that time rum was also produced in New York and New England from molasses imported from the West Indies. Another important Caribbean island for the production of rum is Jamaica, that traditionally double-distilled its rum in still-pots. Martinique, Barbados, Dominica, Trinidad and French Guiana are all in their own right well known for their specific types of rum. Rum from the British Virgin Islands was formerly exclusively sold to the British Navy and used for the Royal Navy's daily ration of rum amongst its sailors: a long tradition which lasted until 1970.

❧❧❧ ⟨⟩ ❧❧❧

THE GRUB-STREET JOURNAL, 16 MARCH 1731

Advertisement

Whereas other *Coffee-Houses*, and other *Publick Houses*, take of their Customers 8s. for a Quart of Arrack, and 6s. for a Quart of Rum or Brandy made into Punch, so that it is now become the settled Price throughout the Town, and seldom less than a Bowl of 1s. 6d, is to be had: Therefore, for the better accommodation all Gentlemen, that are Lovers of Punch,

THIS IS TO GIVE NOTICE,

That I have opened on Ludgate-hill, the *London-Coffee-House* and *Punch-House*, (Two *Punch-Bowls* on Iron Pedestals before my Door,)

Where the finest and best old Batavia Arrack, Jamaica Rum, and French Brandy, are made into *Punch*, with the finest Ingredients, viz.

A Quart of Arrack made into *Punch* for 6s. and so in Proportion to the smallest Quantity, which is half a Quartern for 3d. And Gentlemen may have it as soon made as a Gill of Wine can be drawn, with the best of Eating, Attendance, and Accommodation.

This Undertaking has occasion'd many, whose *Interest* it is to possess Gentlemen with such an Opinion, that the Liquors by me used are not good. The Publick is hereby assured, that I buy my Goods on the Keys, and at the best Hand, with Ready Money, and am at this Time provided with as well-chosen Brandies, Rum and Arrack, as any in Town, and will at all times procure the best that is imported. But what may convince Gentlemen of the Truth hereof, is, (not only by Encouragement I meet with) that the Sherbet is always brought by itself, and the Brandy, Rum, or Arrack in the Measure, so there can be no Imposition, either in Quantity or Quality; for the Proof whereof I appeal to all Gentlemen who have done me the Honour to call at my House.

James Ashley

POOR RICHARD'S ALMANAK, 1737

"Boy, bring a Bowl of China here,
Fill it with Water cool and clear:
Decanter with Jamaica right,
And Spoon of Silver clean and bright,
Sugar twice-fin'd, in pieces cut,
Knife, Sieve and Glass, in order put,
Bring forth the fragrant Fruit, and then
We're happy till the Clock strikes Ten."

Supper of Brotherly Love

BROTHERLY LOVE IN DISGUISE

~

PHILADELPHIA PEPPER POT

~

PENNSYLVANIA DUTCH SHOO FLY PIE

~

ROYAL CIDER

On an early Sunday morning in 1723 Benjamin Franklin landed at Market Street wharf in Philadelphia, the City of Brotherly Love, to start his new life.

"I was dirty from my Journey; my Pockets were stuff'd out with Shirts and Stockings; I knew no Soul, nor where to look for Lodging. I was fatigu'd with Travelling, Rowing and Want of Rest. I was hungry, and my whole Stock of Cash consisted of a Dutch Dollar and about a Shilling in Copper. The latter I gave to the People of the Boat for my Passage, who at first refus'd it on Account of my Rowing; but I insisted on their taking it, a Man being sometimes more generous when he has but a little Money than when he has plenty, perhaps thro' Fear of being thought to have but little.

Then I walk'd up the Street, gazing about, till near the Market House I met a Boy with Bread. I had made many a Meal on Bread, and inquiring where he got it, I went immediately to the Baker's he directed me to in second Street; and I ask'd for Bisket, intending such as we had in Boston, but they it seems were not made in Philadelphia, then I ask'd for a threepenny Loaf, and was told they had none such; so not considering or knowing the Difference of Money and the greater Cheapness nor the Names of his Bread, I bad him give me three penny worth of any sort. He gave me accordingly three great Puffy Rolls. I was surpriz'd at the Quantity, but took it, and having no room in my Pockets, walk'd off, with a Roll under each Arm, and eating the other. Thus I went up Market Street as far as fourth Street, passing by the Door of Mr. Read, my future Wife's Father, when she standing at the Door saw me, and thought I made, as I certainly did, a most awkward ridiculous Appearance. Then I turn'd and went down Chestnut Street and part of Walnut Street, eating my Roll all the Way, and coming round found my self again at market Street Wharf, near the Boat I came in, to which I went for a Draught of the River Water, and being fill'd with one of my Rolls, gave the other two to a Woman and her Child that came down the River in the Boat with us and were waiting to go farther. Thus refresh'd I walk'd again up the Street, which by this time had many clean dress'd People in it who were all walking the same Way; I join'd them, and thereby was led into the great Meeting House of the Quakers near Market. I sat down among them, and after looking round a while and hearing nothing said, being very drowsy thro' Labour and want of Rest the preceding Night, I fell fast asleep, and continu'd so till the Meeting broke up, when one was kind enough to rouse me. This was therefore the first House I was in or slept in, in Philadelphia."

Brotherly Love in Disguise

4 calves' hearts ~ ½ lb veal forcemeat ~ 10–12 rashers fat bacon
4 oz vermicelli ~ 2 oz fresh breadcrumbs ~ 1 egg ~ 2 oz lard

Cut flaps, gristle and tubes from the hearts and snip out the membranes which divide the heart's inside. Soak in cold water for 2 hours, then wash and soak in fresh water for another 30 minutes. Stuff the hearts with veal forcemeat and sew up the opening with fine string. Wrap the bacon rashers around the hearts and secure them with wooden skewers. Put them in foil and bake in a 350 F (gas mark 4) oven for 1½ hours.

Break the vermicelli into small pieces and boil them in salted water until they are soft. Drain, cool and mix with the breadcrumbs. Remove the hearts from the oven, let them cool off slightly and brush them with a beaten egg. Coat the hearts with the vermicelli and breadcrumb mixture. Return the hearts without the foil to a roasting tray, add the lard and bake at the same temperature for 30 minutes more, or until the coating is crispy and brown.

Philadelphia Pepper Pot

In the bitterly cold winter of 1777–78, farmers in the vicinity of Philadelphia preferred to sell their produce of fresh pork, goose, turkey, skinned potatoes, Indian meal, sauerkraut, leaf tobacco, turnips, milk, cider and beer to the British troops for hard cash rather than accepting the depreciated continental paper currency offered by soldiers from General Washington's army billeted nearby in huts to the west of the Shuylkill. When hard liquor was available to Washington's men at Valley Forge, the most popular recreation was drinking and singing. An estimated 35,000 pounds of meat and 170 barrels of flour per day were needed to feed the Patriots. Throughout the winter and early spring foraging expeditions were frequently sent into the surrounding countryside by George Washington to round up food supplies, however meagre they were, and these expeditions were often unsuccessful. Here in the days of the American Revolution, while Benjamin Franklin was representing the new-born nation in Paris, trying to negotiate a peace treaty with Britain, George Washington's soldiers were waiting to fight the British, and struggling to stay alive. They survived on a scavenged stew called Pepper Pot, in those days made with tripe and vegetables, or on whatever the foraging parties could lay their hands on. The Continental Congress had assured George Washington during that difficult winter at Valley Forge that food and clothing would be sent, but those assurances were not fulfilled. As one of Washington's soldiers wrote to his mother:

> "Cap't Morgan told us that tomorrow we would move to a place called Valley Forge on up the Shuylkill from our camp. It is getting cold now. Snowed a little last night and we kept warm by standing next to the cooking fire."

2 lbs diced chicken thighs and legs ~ 1 lb stewing beef
1 cup carrots, sliced ~ 1 cup celery, sliced ~ 2 large onions,
quartered and sliced ~ 1 fennel, sliced ~ 4 yams, diced
6 cloves chopped garlic ~ 1 red bell pepper (sweet red pepper)
1 green bell pepper (sweet green pepper) ~ 1 cup flour
2 teaspoons ground black pepper ~ 2 teaspoons salt
1 teaspoon Cayenne pepper ~ 1 teaspoon allspice ~ 1 teaspoon mace
1 teaspoon cinnamon ~ 2 tablespoons Worcestershire sauce
1 teaspoon Tabasco ~ 4 star anises ~ 4 bay leaves
1 cup chicken stock (see p. 46) ~ 1 cup red wine ~ 8 tablespoons olive oil

Heat the olive oil in a large casserole, while mixing together the flour, ground black pepper, salt and Cayenne pepper. Roll the diced chicken through this mixture and brown in the olive oil for 10 minutes, or until golden brown and crispy. Take the chicken out and drain. Add the beef to the olive oil and brown on all sides. Add the garlic and onions until the garlic is browned and pour in the chicken stock, red wine, more salt and pepper, allspice, mace, cinnamon, star anise, bay leaves, Worcestershire sauce, and Tabasco, followed immediately by the yams and the carrots. Stir and leave to simmer, covered, for two hours or until the meat is fully cooked and starts to disintegrate. Dice the bell peppers and add to the stew, with the celery and fennel. Add the chicken pieces, stir and leave to simmer for another half-hour, until the stew is nice and thick.

Pennsylvania Dutch Shoo Fly Pie

½ cup butter ~ 1½ cups flour ~ 1 cup brown sugar
1 cup molasses ~ 1 egg, beaten ~ ¾ cup boiling water
1 teaspoon baking soda

Stir molasses, beaten egg, boiling water and baking soda together in a bowl into a smooth liquid mixture. Pour mixture in a 9-inch unbaked pie shell. Mix butter, flour and brown sugar with your hands in a bowl to a consistent crumble. Sprinkle the crumble over the liquid in the pie shell and bake in a 400°F oven (gas mark 6) for 15 minutes. Bake then in a 350°F (gas mark 4) oven for around 30 minutes until the filling has set.

Royal Cider

By 1752 it was estimated there were at least 120 taverns in Philadelphia. Royal Cyder, new cider fermented with applejack, was a favourite tipple in the Red Lion in Elbow Lane, the Pewter Platter off Market Street and the Crooked Billet by Chestnut Street Wharf.

In 1758 Benjamin Franklin wrote from London to Charles Norris, a wealthy Pennsylvanian merchant:

"I hope the Crab Apple Trees you have planted will grow, and be propagated in our Country. I do not find that England any where produces Cyder of equal Goodness with what I drank frequently in Virginia made from those Crabs. They are also said to be plentiful Bearers, and seldom fail. I should be glad to see the Industry of our People supplying the Neighbouring Colonies with Cyder. I think it would even be valued here."

"After all your Apples are bruis'd, take Half of your Quantity and squeeze them, and the Juice you press from them pour upon the others Half bruis'd, but not squeez'd, in a Tub for the Purpose, having a Tap at the Bottom. Let the Juice remain upon the Apples three or four Days, then pull out your Tap, and let your Juice run into some other Vessel set under the Tub to receive it. And if it runs thick, as at the first it will, pour it upon the Apples again, till you see it run clear. And as you have a Quantity, pour it into your Vessel, but do not force the Cyder, but let it drop as long as it will of its own Accord. Having done this, after you perceive that the Sides begin to work, take a Quantity of Ising-glass, an Ounce will serve forty Gallons, infuse this into some of the Cyder till it be dissolv'd. Put to an Ounce of Ising-glass a Quart of Cyder, and when it is so dissolv'd, pour it into the Vessel, and stop it close for two Days, or something more. The draw off the Cyder into another Vessel: this do so often till you perceive your Cyder to be free from all manner of Sediment, that may make it ferment and fret itself: after Christmas you may boil it; you may, by pouring Water on the Apples, and pressing them, make a pretty small Cyder. If it be thick and muddy, by using Ising-glass, you may make it as clear as the Rest. You must dissolve the Ising-glass over the Fire, till it be Jelly."

[SALT]

Salt was first known to be used in ancient history, around 2700 BC, when the *Peng-Tzao-Kan-mu* was published in China. It was most probably the earliest known writing on pharmacology. The major part of this work discussed over 40 different kinds of salt, with methods of extracting and putting them to use. In ancient Greece salt was used as a currency in the slave trade, whence the expression: "not worth his salt". Early Roman soldiers were partially paid in salt, known as *salarium argentum*, from which we gain the English word "salary". As early as 500 years before the arrival of European settlers American Indians were mining salt in Louisiana by boiling brine from salt springs. The Onondaga Indians in New York did likewise in the 1600s. In Colonial America the first patent issued by the British Crown was given to Samuel Winslow of the Massachusetts Bay Company, allowing him the exclusive rights to produce salt for ten years according to his specific methods. In 1776 Lord Howe was appointed Commander of the British fleet during the War of Independence and a year later in 1777 he triumphantly captured the salt supply of General George Washington. The so-called "solar salt" was produced by building sheds over salt pans, protecting them from the rain. First in the 1770s in the San Francisco Bay area and later in the 1800s at the Great Salt Lake in Utah. In 1825, when the Erie Canal was opened, it was dubbed "the ditch that salt built", because salt was its original cargo and was bulky and difficult to transport. Syracuse is still called "Salt City". In the 1830s there were 442 salt works on Cape Cod, while during the Civil War in 1862 full-scale production was started in open quarries and later in 1869 the first underground mine was started with a shaft. Underground salt mining continues today in North America, from Louisiana and Texas in the south to Ontario, Quebec, New Brunswick and Nova Scotia in the north.

[PEPPER]

Pepper originated in Java, India and the Sunda Islands and was the first eastern spice to be introduced to Europe by Arab traders during the Middle Ages. Pepper was then extremely rare and very expensive. It was sometimes even used as a foreign exchange mechanism or as an alternative to paying taxes and ransoms. Black pepper (*piper nigrum*) is a perennial climbing shrub which bears tiny berries, "peppercorns". The same berries also give us white and green peppercorns, depending on how long they are left to ripen on the vine. Black pepper is what you get when the berries are picked green and spread out in the sun to dry, slowly turning from green to dark brown, to black. To obtain white pepper, you let the berry reach full ripeness on the vine (they turn red). The berries are then soaked in water and the outer skin and pulp are removed before allowing them to dry. When the Arab monopoly of the spice trade declined, European nations started to compete for this trade. First were the Spanish and Portuguese, whose mariners like Columbus, Magellan and Vasco da Gama enjoyed virtual supremacy. In 1494, the monarchs of Spain and Portugal accepted two papal bulls sanctioning the division of the New World between them. Later England and Holland successfully challenged their dominion.

In 1701, the Boston-born Englishman Elihu Yale, who had worked in India for the East India Company and later became governor of Madras, donated money through the sale of some of his spice-trade effects to a college in Saybrook, Connecticut. The college afterwards moved to New Haven, where in 1718 it became Yale College in honour of its benefactor.

The Antediluvians were all very sober
For they had no Wine, and they brew'd no October;
All wicked, bad Livers, on Mischief still thinking,
For there can't be good Living where there is not good Drinking

Derry down

'Twas honest old Noah first planted the Vine,
And mended his Morals by drinking its Wine;
Thenceforth as unwholesome he Water decry'd;
For he saw that by drinking it Millions had dy'd.

Derry down

From this Piece of History plainly we find
That Water's good neither for Body or Mind;
That Virtue and Safety in Wine-bibbing's found
While all that drink Water deserve to be drown'd.

Derry down

BENJAMIN FRANKLIN

Bonhomme Parmentier

CREAMED POTATO SOUP

~

POTATO SALAD

~

POMMES DE POISSON

~

PARMENTIER BREAD

~

POTATO PUDDING

Throughout the 18th century France had been plagued by natural disasters: severe rain and hail storms, followed by droughts and icy winters. Crops were destroyed, resulting in hunger and starvation. Frozen rivers stopped the water mills grinding the grain into flour and hampered the transportation of food supplies to the towns. In parts of the country people were forced to boil tree bark to make gruel to feed themselves. During Benjamin Franklin's stay in France he received the following letter from Antoine-Alexis Cadet de Vaux, chemist and pharmacist:

8 October, 1778

Dear Doctor,

I have the honour to send you potato bread, made without a single atom of flour and without mixture of any other foreign substance.

This discovery, so valuable and important, has been made by a Mr Parmentier, my colleague and my friend; both united on this subject, we are now looking to take this into perfection, though it is very sensitive, and to ensure it to be, during shortages, a resource for humanity.

This bread differs a bit from formal bread by its whiteness, its flavour, its lightness and has the benefit of neither mill nor miller; I am not talking about the easiness by which the potato can grow, the price it receives; the white shouldn't cost more than 1 shilling and 6 pence and the grey hardly retails for 9 deniers.

I would like to receive the honour to court you, Sir, and to go into the details that you might have on this subject, which can only be of interest to a philosopher, a friend of man, and a legislator like you.

I am, with the deepest respect, and the sincerest admiration Sir, Your most humble and obedient servant.

Cadet the Younger

P. S. This bread has been quickly baked in the oven, which makes it less attractive to the eye, less than ideal circumstances.

I have taken the liberty to add a second bread which I would like to ask Mr Franklin to pass on to Mrs Helvetius: it shall be better spent on her.

Cadet, potato bread

In 18th-century France potatoes were avoided like the plague, despite efforts by Marie-Antoinette to make the potato more fashionable by wearing potato blossoms in her hair. However, the French pharmacist Antoine Augustin Parmentier believed the potato could be the answer to French farming and grew potatoes in his experimental fields. His efforts to promote the potato to other farmers were met with reservations. They were not very convinced of the benefits of the potato, which they used as cattle food. Parmentier often mentioned the name of Michel Jean de Crèvecœur in his writings, the latter was a Frenchman from Normandy who, at an early age, had emigrated to Canada and later settled as a farmer in upstate New York. Under the name of Hector Saint-Jean de Crèvecœur he wrote a best-selling book called *Letters from an American Farmer* (1782) and under the pseudonym of "Normannus Americanus" he wrote a pamphlet on growing potatoes in the American colonies. Benjamin Franklin suggested that Parmentier should hold a banquet at Les Invalides with potatoes in every course, including a fake fish dish made of potatoes. The idolized Dr Franklin, always wearing his marten fur cap, attended as the guest of honour. He feasted on every course and gave it a rave review. Interestingly enough, it was also during this time that the English habit of grilling beef made its entrée into French cuisine, hence the famous French *steak pommes frites*.

[91]

Creamed Potato Soup

8 large potatoes, peeled and diced ~ 1 teaspoon nutmeg
2 tablespoons butter ~ 1 teaspoon sugar ~ 1 tablespoon salt
2 teaspoons pepper ~ 4 pints of stock ~ 4 egg yolks
2 tablespoons soured cream

Boil the diced potatoes in salted water for about 30 minutes. Drain them and mash them in a casserole with the butter and add the stock. Bring to a boil and add sugar, nutmeg, salt and pepper, while still stirring. Simmer and stir in the egg yolks. Finish off with soured cream and garnish with a handful of chopped parsley.

Potato Salad

1 lb baby potatoes ~ 1 apple ~ ½ cup chopped pickles/gherkins
1 cup coarsely-chopped onions ~ 3 tablespoons mayonnaise
1 teaspoon Dijon mustard ~ 1 tablespoon olive oil ~ 1 tablespoon vinegar
¼ cup chopped parsley ~ pepper and salt

Boil potatoes for 15 minutes, let them cool off and quarter them. Peel, core and slice apple. Mix quartered potatoes, slices of apple, chopped onions, and chopped pickles/gherkins. Add Dijon mustard, olive oil, vinegar and pepper and salt to the mayonnaise and mix homogeneously. Blend mayonnaise mixture into the potato, apple, pickle/gherkin and onion salad. Garnish with chopped parsley.

Pommes de Poisson

1 lb sweet potatoes (yams) ~ 1 lb boiling potatoes
1 tablespoon crushed anchovy ~ 2 eggs ~ 3 tablespoons butter
1 teaspoon pepper

Boil potatoes in their skins for 20 minutes. Drain and peel then. Mash or sieve the potatoes. Blend in butter, pepper and anchovies. Beat the eggs and blend slowly into the mixture, reserving some for glazing. Cool the mixture and spoon it into a greased fish mould or pipe it onto a greased baking tray in the form of a fish. Carve in the scales, fins, eye, mouth, etc. Brush the remaining egg over the fish and bake in a 400°F (gas mark 6) oven for 20–30 minutes till golden brown. Serve with lemon wedges and parsley sprigs.

"Fish and houseguests stink after three days"   BENJAMIN FRANKLIN

Parmentier Bread

2 teaspoons dried yeast ~ 1 teaspoon sugar
2 cups warm water ~ 6 cups potato flour
2 teaspoons salt

Dissolve the sugar in water in a glass bowl and whisk in the dried yeast. Cover the bowl and leave in a warm place for 15 minutes. Sift the potato flour and salt into a mixing bowl and make a hole in the middle. Pour in the yeast mixture and stir gradually, blending in the potato flour from the side. Add more water and knead with your hands until you have a smooth, soft dough. Knead for 10 minutes more on a potato-floured board, wrap loosely in greaseproof paper and leave to rise in a warm place for 1 hour or more, until it is twice the original size. When risen, knock down the dough and knead for 10 more minutes until smooth. Bake in a preheated oven at 400°F (gas mark 6) for 45 minutes.

Potato Pudding

1 quart potatoes ~ ½ lb fresh butter (melted)
6 eggs (beaten) ~ ½ lb fine sugar ~ ½ lb currants ~ 1 glass brandy
1 glass white wine

"Take the quart of Potatoes, boil them soft, peel them and mash them with the Back of a Spoon. Rub them through a Sieve, to have them fine and smooth; take Half a Pound of fresh Butter melted, Half a Pound of fine Sugar, so beat them well together till they are very smooth, beat six Eggs, Whites and all, stir them in, and a Glass of Brandy. You may then add Half a Pound of Currants, boil it Half an Hour, melt Butter with a Glass of White Wine; sweeten with Sugar, and pour over it. You my bake it in a Dish, with Puff-paste all round the Dish and at the Bottom."

Tuesday 20th October 1778

Dear Doctor,

The Deputy General of the Police accepts Thursday the 29th of this month, the day that you have chosen to meet at the hotel Royal des Invalides; I shall have the honour to collect you in the morning, and to accompany you. We shall not only concern ourselves with potato bread, but with all the relative disciplines of the art of baking, which is far from perfection, especially amongst the English; and that our dear American allies can take them with them, and pass on the work of Mr Parmentier, which this chemist shall have the honour of presenting to you.

I am with the deepest respect, Doctor, you very humble and obedient servant.
Cadet the Younger

Potato Vodka

1 jigger potato vodka ~ 1 teaspoon lemon juice ~ 1 mint leaf

Keep a bottle of potato vodka in the freezer, with little shot glasses. Mix the vodka and lemon juice over ice and serve in the frosted glasses during the meal. Decorate with a mint leaf in each glass.

[POTATOES]

Potatoes came to Europe from the Andean mountains of South America, where over two hundred varieties were cultivated at elevations over 10,000 feet. The Inca Indians held the potato in high esteem and valued it not only as a nourishing staple, but also as a measure of time. The time units correlated with the cooking time of the potato.

When the potatoes were introduced to Europe by the explorer Pizzaro in the first half of the 16th century, they were not very well received. Potatoes were believed to cause leprosy, tuberculosis and rickets. The Scots refused to eat them, because potatoes were not mentioned in the Bible. The potato remained tainted by association, despite the efforts by Louis XVI and Marie-Antoinette, who were convinced potatoes should be admired and grew potatoes experimentally at Les Sablons in Neuilly. To protect the tubers the king placed royal guards on watch in the fields with fixed bayonets. Efforts to make the potato more popular and combat famine turned the potato into peasant food, making it a necessary but dull staple. The French politician, writer and gastronome Anthelme Brillat-Savarin, who wrote *Physiologie du goût* (1825) stated: "I appreciate the potato only as a protection against famine; except for that I know of nothing more eminently tasteless".

[VODKA]

Vodka originated somewhere in northern and eastern Europe and arrived in Russia in the early 14th century. In the 1550s Ivan the Terrible established his own monopoly of vodka-distilling taverns, and put a ban on distilling by rivals. This way the vodka profits were guaranteed to roll straight into his imperial coffers.

He needed the support of the Russian nobility, of course, and allowed them to continue producing vodka by turning a blind eye. By the late 17th century Russian vodka taverns outnumbered bathhouses. Around this time vodka became the customary drink at Russian Imperial banquets and Tsar Peter the Great was renowned for his love of vodka during his lavish feasts. The technique of distilling did not reach Russia from the west until the 15th century; previously the Russians produced the strong spirit by freezing the fermented liquid during their cold winters. Because water and alcohol freeze at different temperatures, they were able to produce a stronger drink than by fermentation alone. Vodka was made from natural resources, such as wheat, barley, potatoes, rye, and even rice. The potato is still used in the production of some vodkas, but most of them nowadays are made from grain and corn.

Special Delivery

THE HORSE AND OYSTERS

~

SMOKED SALMON

~

HAND-STAMPED SMOKED GOOSE

~

STEWED PLUMS

August 10th: 1753

Ordered that Mr. Benjamin Franklin, of Philadelphia, in Pennsylvania, and Mr. William Hunter of Williamsburgh, in Virginia, be appointed Deputy Postmasters and Managers of all of his Majesty's Provinces and Dominions, on the Continent of North America, in stead of Elliott Benger Esqr: Deceased, to commence this day, at an Allowance or Salary of £600 per annum to be paid out of the Money arrising from the Postage of Letters passing and repassing through the said Provinces and Dominions of North America.

In 1765, however, the postal service in the American Colonies was divided in a northern district and a southern district. Until then Benjamin Franklin had been Deputy Postmaster of all of North America, but under this new administrative system he became Deputy Postmaster of only the northern district, from Virginia in the south, as far as Canada in the north.

Cravenstreet July 13. 1765

Mr Franklin begs Leave to present his dutiful Respects, and his Congratulations to Lord Bessborough on his Return to the Post-Office. Would have waited on his Lordship, but that he is confined with a little Fit of the Gout.

Genl. Post Office 18 July 1765

Mr Todd presents his Compliments to Mr. Franklin and acquaints him that Lord Bessborough and Lord Grantham meet at the Office on Friday at noon to open their Patent.

September 25, 1765

The Right Honourable William Earl of Bessborough and The Right Honourable Thomas Lord Grantham, His Majesty's Post Master-General of all His Majesty's Dominions in Europe, Africa and America.
To all to whom these presents shall come Greeting.
 Know Ye, That We the said William Earl of Bessborough and Thomas Lord Grantham reposing especial Trust and Confidence in Benjamin Franklin of Philadelphia and John Foxcroft of New York, Esquires, and having received good Testimony of their Fidelity and Loyalty to His Majesty, and of their Ability and Sufficiency, to manage and better regulate the Posts on the Continent of North America, and of their Inclination and Capacity to improve and advance His Majesty's revenues therein, do, by these presents, nominate, depute, constitute, authorize and appoint them the said Benjamin Franklin and John Foxcroft, and the Survivor of them, Our Deputy Postmasters and Managers of the Post in all His Majesty's Provinces and Dominions on the said Continent of North America, except No. Carolina, South Carolina, Georgia, East Florida, West Florida, the Bahama Islands and their Dependencies, To have, hold, exercise and enjoy, the said Office, with all other Powers, Privileges, Profits, Advantages, and Authorities thereunto belonging unto them the said Benjamin Franklin and John Foxcroft and the Survivor of them, from the Day of the date hereof, for and during the Term of three Years, or 'till they receive a new Commission from Us, or 'till this present Commission be superseded. And We do hereby strictly require all Officers and others employed in or about the Posts already settled or to be settled, in any Part of His Majesty's said Provinces and Dominions in North America, except as before excepted, or in relation to the Revenue arising by the Post of Letters there, from time to time, to give an Account of their Doings and Transactions therein to the said Benjamin Franklin and John Foxcroft, and the Survivor of them, and to observe and obey their Orders and Directions, in relation to their respective Offices, Trusts, and Imployments; And the better to enable the said Benjamin Franklin and John Foxcroft and the Survivor of them, to execute the Office and Trust reposed in them; We do hereby delegate unto them or either of them, all Our Power and Authority to appoint sufficient Deputies, Officers or Agents under them for the better managing and ordering the said Posts in North America; And for collecting and improving the Revenue arising hereby, granting them full Power and

Authority so far as by Law We can, to suspend, remove or displace such Deputies, Officers, or Agents, and all or every other Person or Persons whatsoever employed, or to be employed, in the Management of the said Posts, or in the Collection of the said Revenue, who shall be guilty of any Neglect, Mismanagement, or Breach of Duty in their respective Offices, or Employments, from the farther Execution of his or their Offices, And We do hereby authorize and empower them the said Benjamin Franklin and John Foxcroft and the Survivor of them, to allott, order, and settle from time to time, the Salaries or Allowances which each Deputy, Officer or Agent, who shall be employed in or about the said Posts, shall be paid for their Trouble, Care, or Charge in their respective Offices, And We do also, hereby, grant, and appoint unto them the said Benjamin Franklin, and John Foxcroft and the Survivor of them for their Care, Pains and Trouble, in the Performance and Execution of the Office and Trust hereby granted and committed unto them the Yearly Salary of Six hundred Pounds to commence from the date hereof, which Salary they are to receive or be allowed in their Accounts, out of the Revenue arising to His Majesty, by the Post of Letters within the said Provinces and Dominions in North America.

In Witness whereof We the said William Earl of Bessborough and Thomas Lord Grantham have hereunto set Our Hands, and caused the Seal of our Office to be affixed, this Twenty fifth day of September in the Year of Our Lord One Thousand seven Hundred and Sixty five, in the Fifth Year of His Majesty's Reign.

Bessborough
Grantham

By Command
Henry Potts Secy.
B. Franklin and John Foxcroft

As Deputy Postmaster in the Colonies, Benjamin Franklin was in charge of designing routes for the delivery of the mail. When setting out in his carriage to measure the routes, he had his own new invention in the form of a simple odometer attached to his carriage, to keep track of the distances. Under his stewardship, Benjamin Franklin improved the service immensely by extending it to the newly obtained French holdings in Canada. Voltaire scornfully dismissed the loss of French territory in Canada as a "few acres of snow". Benjamin Franklin also set out on a series of postal inspections and brought the service between New York and Boston down from three weeks to six days, as he had earlier done between New York and Philadelphia. Benjamin Franklin paid a visit to all major towns in New England. One day riding into Hartford, he pulled into an inn, where he found all the chairs around the hearth were taken. He gave the innkeeper an order for "a bucket of oysters for my horse". He then repeated his order to the astonished innkeeper and all the other guests vacated their seats by the fire and went outside to witness a horse that ate oysters. A few instances later the innkeeper and guests rushed back inside. "Your horse won't eat the oysters!" "In that case," said Benjamin Franklin from his seat by the warming hearth, "I'll have the oysters and give my horse some hay."

Postmaster was a patronage job, which allowed Franklin to send his *Pennsylvania Gazette* around free of charge. He was also at liberty to appoint members of his family as his deputies in various regions. The Gazette had carried numerous stories of murders, muggings and robberies committed by convicts who were sent to the Colonies by Britain and were prowling the streets of Philadelphia. In 1751, there appeared a letter to the editor in the Gazette written by Benjamin Franklin himself under the pseudonym Americanus:

"By a Passage in one of your late Papers, I understand that the Government at home will not suffer our mistaken Assemblies to make any Law for preventing or discouraging the Importation of Convicts from Great Britain, for this kind of Reason. *'That such Laws are against the Publick Utility, as they tend to prevent the* IMPROVEMENT *and* WELL PEOPLING *of the Colonies.'* Such a tender *parental* Concern in our *Mother Country* for the *Welfare* of her Children, calls aloud for the highest *Returns* of Gratitude and Duty. This every one must be sensible of: But 'tis said, that in our present Circumstances it is absolutely impossible for us to make *such* as are adequate to the Favour. I own it; but nevertheless let us do our Endeavour. 'Tis something to show a grateful Disposition."

In some of the uninhabit'd Parts of these Provinces, there are Numbers of these venomous Reptiles we call RATTLE-SNAKES; Felons-convict from the Beginning of the World: These, whenever we meet them, we put to Death, by Virtue of an old Law, *Thou shalt bruise his Head.* But as this is a sanguinary Law, and may seem too cruel; and as however mischievous those Creatures are with us, they may possibly change their Natures, if they were to change the Climate; I would humbly propose, that this general Sentence of *Death* be changed for *Transportation.*"

In the Spring of the Year, when they first creep out of their Holes, they are feeble, heavy, slow, and easily taken; and if a small Bounty were allow'd *per* Head, some Thousands might be collected annually, and *transported* to Britain. There I would propose to have them carefully distribute'd in St James's Park, in the Spring-Gardens and other Places of Pleasure about London; in the Gardens of all the Nobility and Gentry throughout the Nation; but particularly in the Gardens of the *Prime Ministers*, the *Lords of Trade* and *Members of Parliament*; for to them we are *most particularly* obliged."

There is no human Scheme so perfect, but some Inconveniences may be objected to it: Yet when the Conveniences far exceed, the Scheme is jug'd rational, and fit to be executed. Thus Inconveniences have been objected to that *good* and *wise* Act of Parliament, by virtue of which all the Newgates and Dungeons in Britain are emptied into the Colonies. It has been said, that these Thieves and Villains introduc'd among us, spoil the Morals of Youth in the

Neighbourhoods that entertain them, and perpetrate many horrid Crimes: But let not *private Interests* obstruct *publick Utility*. Our *Mother* knows what is best for us. What is a little *Housebreaking, Shoplifting*, or *Highway Robbing*; what is a *Son* now and then *corrupted* and *hang'd*, a Daughter <u>debauch'd</u> and *pox'd*, a Wife *stabb'd*, a Husband's *Throat cut*, or a Child's *Brains beat out* with an Axe, compar'd with this 'IMPROVEMENT and WELL PEOPLING of the Colonies!' "

Thus it may perhaps be objected to my Scheme, that the *Rattle-Snake* is a mischievous Creature, and that his changing his Nature with the Clime is a mere Supposition, not yet confirm'd by sufficient Facts. What then? Is not Example more prevalent than Precept? And may not the honest rough British Gentry, by a Familiarity with these Reptiles, learn to *creep*, and to *insinuate*, and to *slaver*, and to *wiggle* into Place (and perhaps to *poison* such as stand in their Way) Qualities of no small Advantage to Courtiers! In comparison of which '*Improvement* and *Publick Utility*,' what is a *Child* now and then kill'd by their venomous Bite, —or even a favourite *Lap-Dog?*..."

The Horse and Oysters

12 oysters on the half shell (opened) ~ 3 lemons ~ ½ teaspoon salt
½ teaspoon chilli powder ~ ½ teaspoon dried garlic
½ teaspoon ground star anise ~ ¼ teaspoon ground ginger
¼ teaspoon ground coriander seed ~ ¼ teaspoon ground white pepper
¼ teaspoon ground cinnamon ~ ¼ teaspoon onion powder
¼ teaspoon ground cloves ~ ¼ teaspoon ground cumin

Mix all these finely ground spices together in a pestle and mortar. Cut the lemons into wedges and squeeze the lemon juice generously over the oysters. Dust off the oysters with the mixture of the above spices.

Smoked Salmon

1 lb smoked salmon ~ 1 dozen smoked quails' eggs ~ 4 teaspoons capers
1 cup mayonnaise ~ 1 teaspoon ground black pepper
1 teaspoon Cayenne pepper ~ 8 lemon wedges ~ 6 sprigs of parsley

Unwrap the smoked salmon and slice it as thinly as possible. Cut the smoked quails' eggs in thin slices. Mix the capers thoroughly with the mayonnaise and add the Cayenne pepper. Mix well and set aside. Arrange the slices of smoked salmon on a platter and top with the slices of smoked quails' eggs. Dust with the ground pepper. Chop one sprig of parsley very fine and sprinkle them over the salmon and egg slices. Spoon the mayonnaise with caper mix in the middle, on top of the salmon and decorate with a second sprig of parsley. Arrange the lemon wedges along the side, with the remaining 4 sprigs of parsley. Serve with whole-wheat toast.

Hand-Stamped Smoked Goose

2 breasts of smoked goose ~ 1 egg ~ ½ cup breadcrumbs
1 teaspoon salt ~ 1 teaspoon pepper ~ 4 tablespoons butter
4 lemon wedges ~ ¼ cup chopped parsley

Take a meat pouncer and flatten the smoked goose breasts by hand, until about ½ inch thick. Take a rolling pin and roll out the breasts in all directions, until ¼ inch thick. Beat the egg in a large glass bowl and coat the flattened goose breasts. Season with salt and pepper and coat with the breadcrumbs. Melt the butter in a sauté pan, until very hot, and fry the breasts on both sides, until golden and crispy. Arrange on a platter and sprinkle with chopped parsley and decorate with the lemon wedges. Serve with stewed plums.

Stewed Plums

½ lb purple plums ~ ¼ pint port ~ 3 tablespoons corn syrup
fresh sage leaves

Cut the plums in half, take the stones out, and braise in a saucepan for 5–8 minutes. Stir in the corn syrup, followed by the port and cook until the stew reduces. Serve on the side of the smoked goose breasts.

"Give me yesterday's Bread, this Day's Flesh, and last Year's Cyder"
BENJAMIN FRANKLIN

❦ ❦ ❦

January 31st: 1774

Sir,

I have received the Commands of His Majesty's Post Master General to signify to you that they find it necessary to dismiss You from being any longer Their Deputy for America. You will therefore cause your accounts to be made up as soon as you can conveniently. I am, Sir, Your most humble Servant,

Anth. Todd Secy.

THE PENNSYLVANIA GAZETTE, 1758

"Whereas the News-papers of the several Colonies on this Continent, heretofore permitted to be sent by Post free of Charge, are of late Years so much increased as to become extremely burthensome to the Riders, who demand additional Salaries or Allowances from the Post-Office on that Account; and it is not reasonable, that the Office, which receives no Benefit from the Carriage of News-papers, should be at any Expense for such Carriage: And Whereas the Printers of News-papers complain, that they frequently receive Orders for News-papers from distant Post-Offices, which they comply with by sending the Papers, tho' they know not the Persons to whom the Papers are to be directed, and have no convenient Means of Collecting the Money, so that much of it is lost; and that for Want of due Notice when distant Subscribers die, become Bankrupt, or remove out of the Country, they continue to send Papers some Years directed to such Persons, and the Loss so great to the Printers, as that they cannot afford to make any Allowance to the Riders for carrying the Papers: And whereas some of the Riders do, and others may, demand exhorbitant Rates of Persons living on the Roads, for carrying and delivering the Papers that do not go into any Office, but are delivered by the Riders themselves.

To remedy these Inconveniences, and yet not to discourage the Spreading of News-papers, which are on many Occasions useful to Government, and advantageous to Commerce, and to the Publick; You are, after the first Day of June next, to deliver no News-papers at your Office (except the single Papers exchang'd between Printer and Printer) but to such Persons only as do agree to pay you, for the Use of the Rider which brings such Papers, a small additional Consideration per Annum, for each Paper, over and above the Price of the Papers; that is to say, For any Distance not exceeding Fifty Miles such Paper is carried, the Sum of Nine pence Sterling per Annum, or an Equivalent in Currency."

The Cook's File

FORC'D COCKS-COMBS

~

CHESHIRE PORK PYE FOR SEA

~

MAHI-MAHI

~

OVEN-BAKED RICE PUDDING

The English made an appeal to Benjamin Franklin while he was staying in Passy in 1779. Could he help grant safe passage to Captain Cook, who had sailed out to the Pacific before the War of Independence had broken out. Dr Franklin the scientist sent out an appeal to the revolutionary American Navy:

"To all Captains and Commanders of arm'd Ships acting by Commission from the Congress of the United States of America, now in War with Great Britain.

Gentlemen,   Passy, March 10, 1779

A Ship having been fitted out from England before the Commencement of this War, to make Discoveries of new Countries, in Unknown Seas, under Conduct of that most celebrat'd Navigator and Discoverer Captain Cook; an Undertaking truly laudable in itself, as the Increase of Geographical Knowledge, facilitates the

Communication between distant Nations, in the Exchange of useful Products and Manufactures, and the Extension of Arts, whereby the common Enjoyments of human Life are multiplied and augmented, and Science of other kinds increased to the Benefit of Mankind in general. This is therefore most earnestly to recommend to every one of you; that in case the said Ship which is now expected to be soon in the European Seas on her Return, should happen to fall into your Hands, you would not consider her as an Enemy, nor suffer any Plunder to be made of the Effects contain'd in her, nor obstruct her immediate Return to England, by detaining her or sending her into any other Part of Europe or to America; but that you would treat the said Captain Cook and his People with all Civility and Kindness, affording them, as common Friends to Mankind, all the Assistance in your Power, which they may happen to stand in need of. In doing so you will not only gratify the Generosity of your own Dispositions, but there is no doubt of your obtaining the Approbation of the Congress, and your other American Owners."

By the time Franklin wrote this message of generosity, Captain Cook had already been mortally wounded by natives in 1779 on the Kona coast of the Hawaiian Islands. However, five years later and still residing in Passy, Benjamin Franklin wrote to Viscount Howe in England:

My Lord,

I receiv'd lately the very valuable Voyage of the late Captain Cook, kindly sent to me by your Lordship, in consideration of my Good-Will in issuing Orders towards the Protection of that illustrious Discoverer from any Interruption in his Return home by American Cruisers. The Reward vastly exceeds the small Merit of the Action, which was no more than a Duty to Mankind. I am very sensible of his Majesty's Goodness in permitting the Favor to me, and I desire that my thankful Acknowledgments may be accept'd. With great Respect, I am, my Lord, your Lordship's most obedient and most humble Servant.

B. Franklin.

Forc'd Cocks-Combs

"Parboil your Cocks-Combs, then open them with a Point of a Knife at the Great-end. Take the White of a Fowl, as much Bacon and Beef Marrow, cut these small, and beat them fine in a Marble Mortar. Season them with Salt, Pepper and grated Nutmeg, and mix it with an Egg. Fill the Cocks-Combs, and stew them in a little strong Gravy softly for Half an Hour. Then slice in some fresh Mushrooms, and a few pickled ones. Then beat up the yolk of an Egg and put it to the Gravy, while stirring it. Season it with Salt. Dish them up in little Dishes or Plates."

Cheshire Pork Pye for Sea

"Take some salt Pork that has been boiled, cut it into thin Slices, an equal Quantity of Potatoes pared and sliced thin. Make a good Crust, cover the Dish, lay a Layer of Meat, seasoned with a little Pepper, and a Layer of Potatoes; then a Layer of Meat, a Layer of Potatoes, and so on till your Pye is full. Season it with Pepper; when it is full, lay some Butter on the Top, and fill your Dish above Half full of soft Water. Close your Pye and bake it in a gentle Oven."

Mahi-Mahi

4 mahi-mahi steaks from Hawaii ~ ½ red bell pepper (sweet red pepper)
½ green bell pepper (sweet green pepper)
½ yellow bell pepper (sweet yellow pepper) ~ 1 onion
1 tablespoon crushed garlic ~ 4 tablespoons lemon juice
4 tablespoons lime juice ~ ½ cup olive oil ~ 1 teaspoon salt
1 teaspoon pepper ~ ½ cup fresh whole basil leaves

Rub the mahi-mahi steaks with salt & pepper and marinate in olive oil and the juices of the lemons and limes. Slice the onion and the bell peppers lengthways and sauté with the crushed garlic in olive oil till slightly brown. Charbroil the mahi-mahi steaks over high heat until brown on the outside and just cooked on the inside. Serve on a platter and top with the sautéed coloured peppers and onion. Garnish with the whole basil leaves. Serve with cooked rice.

Oven-Baked Rice Pudding

"Boil a pound of rice until it's tender. Drain it and dry it as much as you can, without squeezing it. Then add a good piece of butter and stir in some sugar to taste. Add a little bit of grated nutmeg, mix it all well, pour it in a dish that is coated with butter and cook it in the oven. You may add some raisins if desired."

[SUGAR]

Sugar cane is a tall tropical perennial of the grass family. It is native to Asia, where it was first cultivated some 10,000 years ago in New Guinea. Sugar cane and sugar beet are the major sources of sugar today. The cane is harvested by cutting down the stalks and pressing them in order to extract the juice, which is then concentrated by evaporation, with syrup, rum and molasses as by-products. The Romans were familiar with the sugar cane and sugar during the first century AD and sugar was first written about in a Hindu religious book around 500 AD, in which the process of boiling the cane juice and making sugar is described. The Moors introduced sugar and its technology to Europe during their occupation of the Iberian peninsula. Sugar was first brought from the Canary Islands to the Americas by Columbus in 1493 and first grown in Hispaniola. The Polynesians also introduced the sugar cane to America when they settled Hawaii. It was used as food sweetener and the stalks were used for wind protection. In the 16th century Portugal, using cane from Brazil was the largest sugar producer. Later in the 18th century it was challenged by the Spanish plantations on Cuba and the British sugar islands of Barbados and Jamaica. Successful Hawaiian sugar cane production began in the mid 1800s following the development of new centrifuge equipment, separating the molasses from the sugar syrup. Benjamin Franklin considered the production of sugar from sugarcane a nasty and filthy process. He described three alternative commodities, Sweet Apple, Red Beet and Sugar Maple, out of which sugar could be made as follows:

"But we have in our Power another Syrup, both pleasant and wholesome, capable of serving all the Family Purposes of Molasses, and more; I mean the Syrup produced by boiling down the express'd Juice of the Sweet Apple, before fermentation, till it comes to a proper Consistence. A Gentleman in Bucks County has, I am informed, practised this some Years, with great Success, plentifully supplying the Demands of his own Family, and having some to spare. It answers some Purposes of Sugar, and does extremely well in Tarts, &c. And even Sugar itself is not quite out of our Power to make, though not from the Sugar Cane. The express'd Juice of red Beets, strained and purified a little, then boiled down to the Consistence of a Syrup. Every two Pound of Beets makes two Ounces and a Half of Sugar. And from the Sugar Maple great Quantities may be made. In the Frontiers of Connecticut they are now much in the Practice of it."

THE PENNSYLVANIA GAZETTE, July 12. 1764

As several Persons, during this very hot Weather, have lost their Lives, by indiscreetly drinking cold Water, while they were warm, and sweating, we think it is our Duty to acquaint the Publick therewith; and to request that every One, before he drinks, will mix a little Spirit with his Water, which should stand some Time after taken from the Pump, as the Consequence, without doing so, seems to be immediate Death. —It is said to be a good Way to keep the Water in the Mouth some Time, before it is swallowed.

Receipt for the Bite of a Mad Dog

"For the Bite of a Mad Dog, for either Man or Beast: Take six Ounces of Rue clean picked and bruised, four Ounces of Garlick peeled and bruised, four Ounces of Venice Treacle, and four Ounces of filed Pewter, or scraped Tin. Boil these in two Quarts of the best Ale, in a Pan covered close over a gentle Fire, for the Space of an Hour, then strain the Ingredients from the Liquor. Give eight or nine Spoonfuls of it warm to a Man, or a Woman, three Mornings fasting. Eight or nine Spoonfuls is sufficient for the strongest; a lesser Quantity to those younger, or a weaker Constitution, as you may judge of their Strength. Ten or twelve Spoonfuls for a Horse, or a Bullock; three, four, or five to a Sheep, Hog, or Dog. This must be given within nine Days after the Bite; it seldom fails in Man or Beast. If you can conveniently bind some of the Ingredients on the Wound, it will be so much the better."

Royal Society Club

POTTED SALMON

~

PIGEON WITH OYSTER STUFFING

~

GRILLED CUTS OF MEAT

~

ROYAL APPLE TURNOVER

~

CHAMPAGNE

A few years before Franklin landed in London in 1757, he had been awarded the Godfrey Copley Medal by the Royal Society for his electrical experiments. The Royal Society was established in London in 1660 by a group of learned men to stimulate and promote scientific research and discussion and was granted a royal charter in 1662. The Copley Medal was the Royal Society's highest yearly award for scientific work. Benjamin Franklin thanked the gentlemen of the Royal Society for his award with his usual wit:

> "The very great Honour you have done me, in adjudging me your Medal for 1753, demands my grateful Acknowledgements, which I beg you would accept as the only Return at present in my Power.
>
> I know not whether any of your learned Body have attain'd the ancient boasted Art of multiplying Gold; but you have certainly found the Art of making it infinitely more valuable."

Soon after his arrival in London in 1757 Franklin was invited to attend a dinner at the Royal Society on 11th August. Here is a bill of fare from a Royal Society dinner of around that time:

Salmon & Smelts ~ Trout & flat Fish ~ Fowls & Bacon ~ Roast Beef
Goose Roast ~ Pidgeon Pye ~ Pease ~ Plumb Pudding
Codling Pye Creamed ~ Haunch of Venison ~ Currant & Cherry Pye
Butter & Cheese

Benjamin Franklin became a Member of Council of the Royal Society and was appointed to a committee in 1772 to study ways to protect the Purfleet gunpowder magazines from lightning strikes.

Benjamin Franklin dined often with John Pringle at the Royal Society Club, which he enjoyed so much for its relaxed and cultured informal atmosphere. His last supper at the club, which he shared with his good friends John Pringle, Cavendish and Joseph Banks, was on 19th January 1775, just two months before he was to leave England for good. Nine years later in 1784, as president of the Royal Society, Sir Joseph Banks, who had accompanied James Cook on an earlier trip around the world, sent Benjamin Franklin the following letter:

"Willing as much as in my power to clear the Royal Society and myself from our share of the charge of illiberal treatment towards you, with which I fear this country may too justly be accused, I take my pen with no small pleasure to inform you, that I am instructed by the Council of the Royal Society, to present to you, in their name, the gold medal which they have struck in honour of Captain Cook, in testimony how truly they respect those liberal sentiments which induced you, upon his return to Europe unexpected, to issue your orders to such American cruisers as were then under your direction, to abstain from molesting that great navigator; an act worthy of those sentiments of general philanthropy by which I have observed your conduct ever actuated since I have had the honour of your acquaintance."

Potted Salmon

8 salmon steaks (6 oz each)
1 oz mixed nutmeg, mace, cloves and white pepper ~ 4 oz butter
4 oz finely chopped onions ~ 6 bay leaves ~ 4 oz clarified butter
6 chopped anchovy fillets

Season the salmon steaks with the mixture of nutmeg, mace, cloves and white pepper. Arrange the steaks in a well-greased baking tray with butter between the layers. Sprinkle with the chopped onions and lay the bay leaves and the chopped anchovy fillets on top. Dot with butter and cover with foil.

Bake in a 350 F (gas mark 4) oven for 30–40 minutes. Lift the salmon out and drain. Remove the skin and bones. Pound or flake the flesh and pack tightly in pots, covered with clarified butter and leave to set.

Pigeon with Oyster Stuffing

1 wood pigeon ~ 1 dozen oysters ~ 2 chopped shallots
1 cup breadcrumbs ~ 1 cup white wine ~ 2 teaspoons capers
2 teaspoons pepper ~ 2 teaspoons salt ~ 6 oz butter ~ 1 sprig of parsley

Rinse pigeon with cold water and pat dry with a towel. Season bird inside and outside. Melt butter in deep casserole and brown bird on all sides. Cover casserole while basting from time to time. To prepare stuffing; shuck oysters, sauté shallots in butter and pigeon drippings till soft and light brown, then add oysters and quickly sauté them till they are just done. Add white wine, breadcrumbs and capers and mix thoroughly till hot. Stir in chopped parsley and fill the cavity of the wood pigeon just 15 minutes before serving the bird. Serve with red cabbage and mashed potatoes.

"Kill no more pigeons than you can eat"   BENJAMIN FRANKLIN

Grilled Cuts of Meat

"First your fire has to be bright and hot; your grill being very clean, put it in the fire; take the cuts of beef and cut them thickly, about half a thumb (inch); sprinkle them with a bit of salt and pepper and place them on the grill. Don't turn your cuts until one side is done being grilled; then when you turn them to their other side, there shall be enough rich sauce on that surface, so that one has to be very careful not to lose it. After your cuts have been grilled enough, take them carefully off the grill, so not to spill any juices and place them on a very hot plate, cover them with another one and carry them to the table. The great delicacy of this dish is to have it very hot and very succulent.

One can (if one wishes) cut very finely on a plate, before putting in the cuts, a shallot or two, or a finely cut onion."

Royal Apple Turnover

4 apples, such as Golden Delicious, Cox, or Newton Pippins
4 oz raisins ~ 2 cups all-purpose flour ~ 6 oz butter
2 tablespoons shortening ~ 5 tablespoons sugar ~ ¼ teaspoon salt
½ cup iced water ~ ½ cup cider ~ 1 teaspoon cinnamon
juice of ½ lemon ~ 1 egg, beaten

Peel, core and quarter the apples. Slice them thinly. Fill a bowl with cold water, cider and lemon juice and mix with the thin apples slices. Stir in the cinnamon and 3 tablespoons sugar. Set aside for 30 minutes.

Sift flour into a bowl with 2 tablespoons sugar and the shortening. Cut the butter quickly into tiny pieces and rub it into the flour mixture. Mix with iced water to form a firm and pliable dough, neither dry and hard nor sticky. Wrap and chill for 1 hour.

Roll out the dough into a rectangular shape (9×18 inches) on a floured surface. Cut away the edges and refrigerate.

Put the dough on a buttered baking tray and place the apple slices and raisins on half the surface. Add a bit more sugar to taste. Flip over the other half of the dough onto the apples and raisins and press the sides with some water to seal. Turn up the three sides and press markings into them with a fork. Take the cutaway dough edges out of the refrigerator and knead into a ball. Roll out the dough several times and cut into ½ inch strips to decorate the top of the turnover and refrigerate for one hour.

Preheat oven to 400°F (gas mark 6). Brush the turnover with some water and brush the turnover with the beaten egg and prick two holes in the top. Place the baking tray in the middle of the pre-heated oven and bake for 40 minutes or until the bottom is brown and steam comes out of the holes.

"Maids of America, who gave you bad teeth?
Answ. Hot Soupings: and frozen Apples"   BENJAMIN FRANKLIN

PENNSYLVANIA GAZETTE 1738

We have the Pleasure of acquainting the World, that the famous Chinese or Tartarian Plant, called Gin seng, is now discovered in this Province, near Sasquehannah: From whence several whole Plants with a Quantity of the Root, have been lately sent to Town, and it appears to agree most exactly with the Description given of it in Chamber's Dictionary, and Pere du Halde's Account of China. The Virtues ascrib'd to this Plant are wonderful.

[CHAMPAGNE]

The first people to grow grapes in the Champagne region were possibly the Celts, who were known to have been wine drinkers. The Romans, for whom wine played an important role in their civilization, introduced vine growing in many corners of their Empire. The earliest recorded history of wine cultivation in Champagne dates from the 9th century, when the Archbishop of Reims recommended wines from Epernay to the ailing Bishop of Laon, for their high restorative character. The abbey of Hautvillers near Epernay grew throughout the Middle Ages and early Renaissance into one of the province's leading monasteries. There in 1668 a young monk known as Dom Pierre Pérignon arrived. The first champagnes did not sparkle and when they did, they were considered failures. White grapes especially had a tendency to have a second fermentation, and Dom Pérignon as the abbey's cellarer, therefore, preferred the dark grape to the white. Gradually the refermented white wines started to gain in popularity and Dom Pérignon eventually began to make them himself. He improved the quality of the grapes and blended them with others, perfected the pressing process, and bottled the wine in stronger bottles with better quality corks. Thus a quality vintage wine was created that would improve over time.

The Roast Beef of Old England

By Richard Leveridge, 1735

When Mighty Roast Beef was the Englishman's Food
It ennobl'd our Veins and enriched our Blood:
Our Soldiers were Brave and our Courtiers were Good:
Oh! The Roast Beef of Old England,
And Old English Roast Beef.

But since we have learned from all vapouring France,
To eat their Ragouts, as well as to Dance.
We are fed up with nothing but vain Complaisance.
Oh! The Roast Beef of Old England,
And Old English Roast Beef.

Our Fathers, of old, were Robust, Stout and Strong,
And kept open House, with good cheer all Day long.
Which made their plump Tenants rejoice in this Song,
Oh! The Roast Beef of Old England,
And Old English Roast Beef.

But now we are dwindled, to what shall I name,
A sneaking poor Race, half begotten ... and Tame,
Who Sully those Honours that once shone in Fame,
Oh! The Roast Beef of Old England,
And Old English Roast Beef.

When good Queen Elizabeth sate on the Throne
E'er Coffee and Tea and such slip-slops were known;
The World was in Terror if e'er she did frown.
Oh! The Roast Beef of Old England,
And Old English Roast Beef.

In those Days, if Fleets did presume on the Main,
They seldom, or never, return'd back again,
As Witness, the Vaunting Armada of Spain.
Oh! The Roast Beef of Old England,
And Old English Roast Beef.

Oh! Then we had Stomachs to eat, and to fight:
And when wrongs were a-cooking to do ourselves right,
But now we're a ... I could, but good Night.
Oh! The Roast Beef of Old England,
And Old English Roast Beef.

Big Cheese

STRING BEAN AND PARMESAN SALAD

~

CHEESE SOUFFLÉ

~

PARMESAN CHEESE CAKE

~

FRANKLIN'S SPRUCE BEER

During the 18th century all kinds of dishes, drinks and ingredients had made their way to England. Soup came from France, green tea from China and dried curry powder and pickled mangoes were introduced from India. Sea turtles were imported from the West Indies, and sago, made from the pith of the palm tree and imported from the Malay archipelago, was used in making puddings. Meat was still very cheap in England and butter was then double the price of beef. Better means of preservation also meant that cheeses could be shipped to faraway places. Cheddar cheeses came to London from the West Country and Stilton from Huntingdonshire. Even Parmesan cheese had made its way up from Italy. Parmesan cheese must have made quite an impact in England in those days, as it caused Benjamin Franklin to write in 1769 to the American botanist John Bartram:

> "It is true many People are fond of Accounts of old Buildings, Monuments, &c. but there is a Number who would be much better pleas'd with such Accounts as you could afford them: And for one I confess that if I could find in any Italian Travels a Receipt for making Parmesan Cheese, it would give me more Satisfaction than a Transcript of any Inscription from any Stone whatever."

String Bean and Parmesan Salad

1 lb string beans ~ ¼ lb Parma ham ~ ½ cup spring onions
2 crushed cloves of garlic ~ 3 tablespoons Parmesan cheese
3 tablespoons olive oil ~ 3 tablespoons lemon juice
1 teaspoon black pepper ~ 1 teaspoon Dijon mustard ~ ½ teaspoon sugar

Clean and trim the string beans. Steam them for 5–7 minutes until they are half cooked. Drain the string beans and leave to cool. Cut the thinly sliced Parma ham into 1-inch strips. Arrange the string beans on a serving platter and sprinkle the strips of Parma ham over them evenly. Mix the crushed garlic with the olive oil, lemon juice and Dijon mustard. Add the sugar and black pepper and mix thoroughly, until the sugar is dissolved. Pour the dressing over the string beans and Parma ham. To finish, cover the string beans lavishly with Parmesan cheese.

Cheese Soufflé

¼ lb grated Cheddar cheese ~ 2 oz grated Parmesan cheese
2 oz butter ~ 2 tablespoons flour ~ 1 cup hot milk
3 egg yolks ~ 5 egg whites ~ 1 teaspoon nutmeg
1 teaspoon mustard powder ~ 1 teaspoon pepper ~ 1 teaspoon salt

Melt the butter in a saucepan and stir in the flour to make a roux. Stir in the nutmeg, mustard powder, pepper and salt. Then beat in the hot milk, to make a thick consistent sauce. Bring to the boil and stir for 1 minute. Remove from the heat and beat in the 3 egg yolks and add the Cheddar cheese and half the Parmesan cheese. Whisk the egg whites with a pinch of salt until they are stiff, and fold them into the mixture. Spoon the mixture into buttered ramekins, about 1/3 full and sprinkle the second half of the Parmesan cheese over the tops. Bake in a moderate oven, 400°F (gas mark 6) for 25 minutes. Serve at once.

Parmesan Cheese Cake

Filling:

8 oz Parmesan cheese ~ 8 oz cream cheese ~ 2 eggs, separated
8 oz sugar ~ 1 tablespoon lemon juice ~ 1 teaspoon lemon zest

Crust:

2 cups cracker crumbs ~ ½ cup chopped walnuts ~ 3 oz butter ~ ¼ cup sugar

Topping:

½ pint heavy cream ~ ½ pint soured cream ~ 2 tablespoons sugar

For the filling, stir together in a glass bowl the cream cheese and Parmesan cheese, with the egg yolks and the sugar. Add the lemon juice and zest. Beat the egg whites until stiff and fold in the cheese mixture.

Blend together the crushed crackers, and chopped walnuts, sugar and melted butter. Pat this mixture into a well-buttered 9-inch pie dish and bake at 350°F (gas mark 4) for 15 minutes.

Pour the cheese mixture on top of the crust and bake again at 350°F (gas mark 4) for 25 to 30 minutes.

Whisk the heavy cream, soured cream and sugar until stiff and serve as topping for the cheese cake.

Franklin's Spruce Beer

"For a Cask containing 80 Bottles, take a Pot of Essence (of Spruce) and 13 Pounds of Molasses – or the same amount of Raw Sugar; mix them well together in 20 Pints of hot Water. Stir until they foam, then pour it into the Cask, which you shall fill with Water: add then a Pint of good Yeast; keep stirring, and let it rest for 2 or 3 Days to ferment, after which you close the Cask, and in a few Days, it will be ready to be put into Bottles, that should be perfectly well-corked. Leave them 10 to 12 Days in a cool Cellar, after which the Beer will be good to drink."

It was four years later in 1773, when Dr Franklin finally received a letter from Dr Leith, who painstakingly explained:

The Parmesan Cheese is not made at present in the neighbourhood of Parma, but is solely the produce of the state of Milan, and especially of the country betwixt Placentia and Milan; that made near Lodi is the most esteemed. The following account is given from an observation of the whole process, as conducted at a considerable Farmer's on the road to Lodi.

The milk of fourscore cows, which had been kept over night, was skimmed about four o'clock in the morning, and at the same time the cows were again milked, and at seven that milk was skimmed; then the skimmed milk of both evening and morning were put together in a large copper vessel, wide at the mouth, gradually diminishing some way down, and towards the bottom it became a perfect cylinder, nearly of the diameter of the cheese they usually make. This vessel was suspended by an iron rod turning on an axis, by means of which it could be put upon, or removed from the fire at pleasure. The milk was then made blood warm, to fit it for the action of the runnet, and removing it from the fire, runnet was put to it in the common way. After waiting an hour, the coagulation was perfect, though the curd was tender, and they then broke it down by means of a stick, with a round board, of six inches in diameter fastened to the end of it; after which they broke it still more, by dividing any lumps that were formed, by a stick, through which a number of twigs were passed in different directions. The curd was then allowed to subside, and about a fifth part of the whey was taken off, and put by in a large pail; after which the vessel was again placed upon the fire, (which never was allowed to become very strong), and kept there for an hour an[d a] half. During all this time, one of the people was constantly employed in stirring and breaking down the curd, as above described.

About half an hour after the vessel had been put upon the fire, a quantity of powdered saffron was put in without any rule but the putting as much as was sufficient to give the whey the tinge of a high-coloured Parmesan Cheese, the curd remaining for some time as white as before. They then heated the whey, so as to render it insufferable for one to retain the hand in it, by which they knew it was proper to turn the vessel from the fire. We observed, that during this process the curd underwent a considerable change; from being spongy, and not easily yielding to pressure, it now seemed to separate spontaneously from the whey, and yielded even to the slightest pressure; we also thought that the whey, in heating, acquired the peculiar smell of Parmesan Cheese. Upon the vessel being removed from the fire, and not stirred, the curd immediately separated very perfectly from the whey, and in less than half an hour they took off all the whey, unless a small pail-full, and it being still pretty hot, a quantity of the cold whey which was first removed, was poured on the curd, by which it was cooled so as to allow a person to raise it from the bottom of the vessel, where it lay already in the form of a cheese; another person then passed a coarse, loosely worked linen cloth under the curd, and brought it round on all sides; then one held the corners of the cloth, whilst another poured back nearly the whole of the whey, in order to facilitate the lifting the curd out of this huge vessel: This was immediately done, and the curd placed in a tub, along with a pail-ful of whey, and after a quarter of an hour it was placed in the mould, which consisted of a single hoop of wood, without either top or bottom, and was only kept in its proper form by means of a cord, so fitted as that by it the size of the mould might be increased or diminished, to adapt it to the quantity of curd.

The ordinary size of the Cheese made there is from two to three feet in diameter, and six to eight inches in thickness. The Cheese was left in the mould, without any weight upon it, for a quarter of an hour, to allow the whey to run out of itself, after which they remove the cloth altogether, and a board of four or five inches in thickness was laid upon it, and some time after a stone, of little more than thirty pounds in weight, was placed above the wood; all this apparatus was removed the day following, and employed for the cheese of that day. The weight being taken off, the cheese was carried into the drying-house, a tolerably cool place, though not so airy as those in this country. The second day they sprinkle some bay salt over it, and it is managed afterwards in the common way, only that when near dry, it is painted over with a substance called Rosette, of a purplish colour.

"The King's cheese is half wasted in parings, but no matter 'tis made of the people's milk"
BENJAMIN FRANKLIN

[CHEESE]

Cheese is believed to have originated in the Middle East, where the story goes of an Arab nomad, who had filled his saddlebag with milk to drink on his journey through the desert. The bag was made from a calf's stomach, which contained rennet that curdles milk. After a day's ride, galloping in the hot sun, the rennin had separated the nomad's milk into whey and curds. Not understanding what exactly had happened, the nomad found the whey very drinkable and he feasted whole-heartedly on the curds. Cheese was known to the Sumerians in ancient Babylonia in 4000 BC and the ancient Greeks had credited Aristaeus, the son of Apollo and Cyrene, with the discovery of cheese. During the Roman Empire cheese making reached a high standard. Ripening processes had been developed and different storing conditions were discovered, resulting in various flavours. Large Roman houses often had a cheese kitchen and big towns a special centre where citizens could have their cheese smoked. Cheese was served on the tables of the Roman nobility and patricians, and travelled with the Roman legions to the far corners of the Empire.

In the Middle Ages the monks became the cheese makers and developed many classic varieties like Munster and Trappiste. Many other new cheeses also came into existence, such as Gorgonzola in 879 or Roquefort in 1070. In the Renaissance came Cheddar in 1500 and Parmesan in 1579, while Gouda and Gloucester were products of the 17th century. Stilton was introduced to the world in 1785 and Camembert in 1791. Cheese became very popular among the French kings and the word *fromage*, which came from the word "formage" (meaning mould or form), has been used for cheese in France since 1180. During a stop at the priory of Rueil-en-Brie, Charlemagne became the first monarch to be introduced to Brie; much later at a banquet during the Vienna Congress (1814–15), Brie was hailed as the "King of Cheeses".

༄༅༅ ༄༅ ༄༅༅

THE PHILADELPHIA GAZETTE. March 15. 1733

Advertisement

Good Rhode-Island CHEESE, and Cod-Fish, sold by the Printer hereof.

Receipt for how to recover the Salt out of old Brine or Pickle, so as to be fit for Use again, and better than at first.

By Benjamin Franklin

Fill an Iron Pot (the broader and shallower, the better) with your Brine or Pickle; mix a sufficient Quantity of Whites of Eggs with the Brine, to clarify it from its Impurities. Boil it at first gently, and when the Scum hath all arisen, take it off carefully. As soon as the Brine is skimmed, abate the Fire, and only retain a moderate Heat, sufficient to keep the Brine of a scalding Heat. When the Brine is fully depurated, add about a tenth Part of sour Whey, which will destroy the corrosive or Eating Quality of the Salt. Keep the Brine of a scalding Heat all the Time the Salt is graining or forming into Crystals. When most of the Water is evaporated, and the Salt chiefly grained, take it from the Fire; and straining it with a Cloth from the remaining Water, you will have a clean and most excellent Salt for Use; which being fine, is fit for the Table; and will moreover preserve Meat good and sound, without corroding or consuming the fat, as common Sea Salt is apt to do.

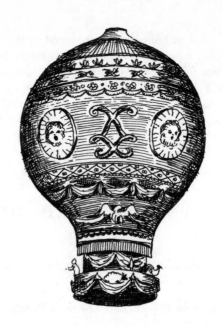

Balloons of Desire

SPINACH SOUP WITH HOT-AIR CROÛTONS

~

FLYING TRINITY

~

FLYING POTATOES

~

MELON BALLOON FRUIT SALAD

In his twilight years in France Benjamin Franklin very keenly followed the craze for ballooning. He travelled from Passy to Paris in 1783 to witness the launching of balloonists like the Montgolfier brothers and Jacques Charles. Several weeks later the Montgolfier brothers ascended in a new hot air balloon in the presence of the French royal family with, as payload, a triple alliance consisting of a duck, a rooster and a sheep. Ten days later, Jacques Charles was in the picture again and took off from the Tuileries in a chariot-shaped gondola suspended below his balloon. He demonstrated he could, to some extent, manoeuvre his craft. Franklin who had contributed financially to this new accomplishment later touched on the question of who was the real father of the balloon, the paper-makers Montgolfier or Charles, the professor?

"Montgolfier the father and Charles the wet-nurse!"

Later in life and troubled by gout, he watched balloon ascents from his house in Passy. In 1785 when the Bostonian Dr John Jeffries made the historical first balloon crossing of the Channel, he carried with him the first batch of international airmail and hand-delivered a letter to Dr Franklin from his son William in England.

Not everyone viewed ballooning so positively as Benjamin Franklin. The English considered the hot air balloon an amusing but useless toy, to which Franklin replied: "What good is a new born baby?"

Benjamin Franklin described these new French experiments with balloons to Sir Joseph Banks of the Royal Society:

"The Morning was foggy, but about one o'Clock the Air became tolerably clear, to the great Satisfaction of the Spectators, who were infinite, Notice having been given of the intended Experiment several Days before in the Papers, so that all Paris was out, either about the Tuileries, on the Quays and Bridges, in the Fields, the Streets, at the Windows, or on the Tops of Houses, besides the Inhabitants of all the Towns and Villages of the Environs. Never before was a philosophical Experiment so magnificently attended. Some Guns were fire'd to give Notice that the Departure of the great Balloon was near, and a small one was discharg'd, which went to an amazing Height, there being but little Wind to make it deviate from its perpendicular Course, and at length the Sight of it was lost. Means were us'd, I am told, to prevent the great Balloon's rising so high as might endanger its Bursting. Several Bags of Sand were taken on board before the Cord that held it down was cut, and the whole Weight being then too much to be lift'd, so a Quantity was discharg'd as to permit its rising slowly. Thus it would sooner arrive at the Region where it would be in equilibrio with the surrounding Air, and by discharging more Sand afterwards, it might go higher if desir'd. Between one and two o'Clock all Eyes were gratifi'd with seeing it rise majestically from among the Trees, and ascend gradually above the Buildings, a most beautiful Spectacle. When it was about two hundred Feet high, the brave Adventurers held out and wav'd a little white Pennant, on both Sides their Car, to salute the Spectators, who return'd loud Claps of Applause. The Wind was very little, so that the Object, though moving northward, continu'd long in view; and it was a great while before the admiring People began to disperse. The Persons embark'd were Mr Charles, professor of experimental Philosophy and a zealous Promotor of that Science; and one of the Messieurs Robert, the very ingenious Constructors of the Machine. When it arriv'd at its Height, which I suppose might be three hundred or four hundred Toises, it appear'd to have only horizontal Motion. I had a Pocket-Glass with which I follow'd it, till I lost Sight, first of the Men, then of the Car, and when I last saw the Balloon it appear'd no bigger than a Walnut.

I write this at seven in the Evening. What became of them is not yet known here. I hope they descend'd by Daylight, so as to see and avoid falling among Trees or on Houses, and that the Experiment was complet'd without any mischievous Accident, which the Novelty of it and the Want of Experience might well occasion. I am the more anxious for the Event, because I am not well inform'd of the Means provid'd for letting themselves gently down, and the Loss of these very ingenious Men would not only be a Discouragement to the Progress of Art, but be a sensible Loss to Science and Society."

Benjamin Franklin foresaw intriguing future applications for ballooning when he wrote to Sir Joseph:

"Among the Pleasantries Conversation produces on this Subject, some suppose Flying to be now invented, and that since Men may be supported in the Air, nothing is wanted but some light handy Instruments to give and direct Motion. Some think Progressive Motion on the Earth may be advanc'd by it, and that a Running Footman or a Horse slung suspended under such a Globe so as to leave no more of Weight pressing the Earth with their Feet, than perhaps 8 or 10 Pounds, might with a fair Wind, and over Hedges, Ditches, and even Waters. It has been even fancied that in time People will keep such Globes anchored in the Air, to which by Pulleys they may draw up Game to be preserved in the Cool, and Water to be frozen when Ice is wanted."

Spinach Soup with Hot-Air Croûtons

1½ lb spinach ~ ½ cup crushed crispy bacon bits ~ 1 cup chapati flour
2 teaspoons nutmeg ~ 1 teaspoon mace ~ 1 teaspoon salt
1 teaspoon ground black pepper ~ 1 large clove finely-crushed garlic
2 tablespoons butter

Mix the chapati flour with water, salt and the finely-crushed garlic. Make it into a dough, roll it out and die-cut ½ inch little circles out of the dough. Clean and wash the spinach and boil with a little water and a pinch of salt in a large pan. When the spinach is half cooked, drain it, keeping the cooking water, and chop as finely as possible (with or without food processor). Melt butter in a large soup pan and add the chopped spinach with the cooking water and the bacon bits. Bring to the heat and add nutmeg, mace, salt, pepper and simmer. Heat cooking oil in a deep pan and deep-fry the chapati rounds, until they puff up into little balloons. Take the balloons out, and drain. Serve the soup in individual bowls and sprinkle the little balloons as *croûtons* into each bowl.

Flying Trinity

½ lb lamb shoulder ~ ½ lb chicken thighs
½ lb duck's breast (preferably *magret* i.e., the lean breast meat of a fatted
mallard or barbary duck with its skin) ~ 1 small courgette (zucchino), sliced
1 small aubergine (eggplant), halved and sliced ~ 6 tablespoons olive oil
4 tablespoons Madeira wine ~ 2 cloves crushed garlic
1 teaspoon salt ~ 1 teaspoon pepper

Cut the lamb, chicken thighs and duck in large chunks and put them in a
marinade of olive oil, crushed garlic, Madeira and salt and pepper for 20
minutes. Alternate the pieces of lamb, chicken, duck with slices of courgette
and aubergine on skewers and brush on a final coating of the marinade.
Preheat a barbecue till the coals are grey and very hot, and charbroil the
skewers until the inside of the meat is just cooked and the outside nice and
golden brown.

Flying Potatoes

1 lb baking potatoes ~ ½ cup olive oil ~ 1 teaspoon salt ~ 1 teaspoon pepper

Wash the potatoes thoroughly and make incisions in each with a knife from
one end, three-quarters of the way through the potato and about ¼ inch
apart. Brush them with olive oil and sprinkle lightly with salt and pepper.
Preheat oven at 400°F (gas mark 6) and bake them till they are well done.

Melon Balloon Fruit Salad

1 ripe cantaloupe ~ 1 ripe honeydew ~ 1 ripe watermelon ~ 2 egg yolks
2 tablespoons of corn syrup ~ ¼ cup whole mint leaves

With a melon scoop round make balls of the cantaloupe, honeydew and
watermelon. Retain the juices. Set the balls in a covered glass bowl to
refrigerate. Whisk the egg yolks in a saucepan and add the corn syrup
slowly, until the mixture thickens. With the mixture in a simmering *bain-marie* then whisk in the retained juices slowly until there is a thick homogeneous sauce. Let the sauce cool off and pour it over the melon balls.
Decorate with whole mint leaves.

"Men and Melons are hard to know"   BENJAMIN FRANKLIN

[OLIVE OIL]

The olive tree (*olea europea*) originates in the Mediterranean. It was first cultivated either by the Syrians or the Minoan civilisation on Crete somewhere between 3500 and 2500 BC. Murals in the palace of Knossos show that the Minoans ate olives and used olive oil for cooking.

Olive tree culture spread to other Mediterranean countries like Greece, Italy and North Africa around 600 BC. Solon enacted special laws protecting the olive tree, Aristotle elevated its cultivation into a science and Hippocrates, the father of medicine, prescribed a spoonful of olive oil as very therapeutic. The olive tree was introduced to the Iberian peninsula by the Phoenicians and Greeks, the Romans and Arabs. Later the Romans extended the production with new techniques. The Roman Empire adored olive oil and considered the consumption of animal fats to be barbaric. The Moors later on perfected the technique of obtaining oil from the olive, thence today's Spanish word for olive oil is "aceite" which is "al-zaita" in Arabic. Olives were taken by the Spanish to the Americas in the 1500s and 1600s and grow in California and parts of Latin America.

THE PENNSYLVANIA GAZETTE, Feb. 3. 1746

To be LETT for Three Years, A Bakehouse, with two ovens, very well situate for carrying on said Trade, being some years standing, and has continual Employ, by loaf bread, brisket baking, and for dinner baking (fixed) fit for any person to go on with said business the first day's entrance. Likewise to be sold or hired, two bolting-mills and chests, with all necessaries whatever for carrying on the business of loaf bread and brisket baking, with two servant lads time, brought up to said business. Any person inclining to purchase, may enter into said business one month after the day of agreement.

For further information, enquire of Benjamin Franklin.

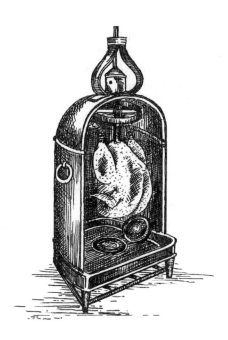

Electrical Fire

BUMPER SOUP BON FRANKLIN

~

ELECTRO-GRILLED TURKEY JOINT

~

OYSTER SAUCE FOR A TURKEY

~

AUBERGINES À LA AMPÈRE

~

BANANES FLAMBÉES

During the 1740s Benjamin Franklin had been introduced to electricity, which was then more of a curiosity and less of a science. In his famous experiment of flying a kite in a thunderstorm, he proved that lightning was electricity. He succeeded in attracting an electric charge from the skies, and demonstrated the existence of positive and negative electricity. The problem of fire damage by lightning was still of great concern in the 18th century. In 1561 Saint Paul's Cathedral in London was struck by lightning and its steeple destroyed. Later, in 1764 London's Saint Bride's church had been hit. The lightning struck the steeple causing an explosion. Stones were hurled higgledy-piggledy into the street.

Lightning rods had to be put on buildings for protection, everybody agreed on that, but the big argument was whether to have blunt rods or pointed rods installed. The Royal Society appointed a committee to investigate whether blunt or pointed conductors should safeguard London's buildings. Benjamin Franklin, as an elected fellow of the Royal Society for his experiments on electricity, was seen as the expert on deciding the right method of protecting the buildings from lightning. His rods were pointed ones and the Royal Society supported him in his decision. King George III, however, entered the controversy by insisting that the Royal Society reverse its recommendation in favour of blunt rods. The President of the Royal Society, Sir John Pringle, also physician to George III, objected, stating the laws of nature could not be reversed. The King demanded Pringle's resignation as President of the Royal Society; he complied. George III went on to have blunt lightning conductors installed on his palace in Kew, which inspired the following epigram by a friend of Benjamin Franklin:

> "While you, great George, for safety hunt,
> And sharp conductors change for blunt,
> The nation's out of joint:
> Franklin a wiser course pursues,
> And all your thunder useless views
> By keeping to the point."

Benjamin Franklin also experimented in killing animals by electrocution, especially turkeys, because that made them so "uncommonly tender". Before electrocution by means of the newly invented "Leyden Jar", animals were killed in the most inhumane way, to keep the meat tender. Living fish were slashed to make the flesh contract. Live lobsters were roasted and eels were skinned alive. Livestock were lashed to death for the same reason and turkeys were suspended by their feet and bled to death.

With the coming of electrocution for slaughtering, the meat would stay tender and the process was more humane—that is to say, as long as nothing went wrong. Benjamin Franklin described an experience with Leyden Jars:

"Two nights ago being about to kill a Turkey from the Shock of two large Glass Jars (Leyden Jars), containing as much electrical fire as forty common Phials, I inadvertently took the whole thro' my own Arm and Body, by receiving the fire from the united Top Wires with one hand, while the other held a Chain connected with the outsides of both Jars. Feeling like a Dead Flesh, I had a Numbness in my Arms and the back of my Neck, which Continued till the Next Morning but wore off. Nothing Remains now of this Shock but a Soreness in my breast Bone."

Peter Collinson, a London merchant and botanist, who had sent Franklin his first Leyden Jar and with whom Franklin kept a lengthy correspondence about his electrical experiments, asked himself the question:

"That the base rubbing of a glass tube should invest a person with electric fire! ... Let him touch spirits of wine & the sparks from his finger on the touch will set the spirits in flame ... I have seen Oyl of Seville oranges & camphor sett fire & Gunpowder mixed with Oyl of Lemons will take fire—but what would you say to see fire come out of a piece of thick ice and set the spirits in flame?"

In one of Benjamin Franklin's many letters to Peter Collinson he ended with a somewhat futuristic view where electricity could be used:

"A Turkey is to be kill'd for our Dinners by the Electrical Shock; and roast'd by the Electrical Jack, before a Fire by the Electrical Bottle; when the Healths of all the famous Electricians in England, France and Germany, are to be drank in Electrical Bumpers, under the Discharge of Guns from the Electrical Battery."

Bumper Soup Bon Franklin

4 cups thinly sliced leeks ~ 3 cups sliced potatoes
4 pints chicken stock (see p. 46) ~ 2 oz butter
2 teaspoons chopped chervil ~ 4 slices of whole wheat bread
2 teaspoons white pepper ~ 2 teaspoons salt

Place the leeks and the potatoes in a casserole and cover with the chicken stock to the brim. Add the white pepper, salt and the butter and put on lid. Simmer gently for several hours. Before serving sprinkle this bumper crop with chopped chervil. Serve with toasted slices of whole wheat bread, neatly cut in half.

Electro-Grilled Turkey Joint

2 turkey legs ~ ½ cup cracked walnuts ~ ½ cup raisins
½ lb pork forcemeat ~ 1 medium sweet onion ~ ½ cup breadcrumbs
1 tablespoon chopped sage ~ 1 tablespoon chopped parsley
2 tablespoons dry sherry ~ 2 tablespoons lemon juice
1 tablespoon butter ~ 2 tablespoons melted butter ~ 1 teaspoon salt
1 teaspoon black pepper

Bone the turkey legs. For the stuffing, chop the onion and fry in butter in a skillet until light golden. Add the forcemeat and stir-fry, while breaking it into pieces. Pour in the sherry and lemon juice while stirring, and mix in the cracked walnuts, raisins, breadcrumbs, chopped parsley and chopped sage. Make sure it becomes of thick consistency. Season generously with black pepper and salt.

Roll out the boned turkey legs and cover with enough stuffing to allow it to be closed. Roll up the stuffed turkey legs and secure tightly with a string. Rub the skin with the melted butter and season with more pepper and salt.

Stick the spit of an electric roasting grill through the two rolled up joints and preheat the grill to 350°F. Grill for 2 hours while the joints keep rotating. Set aside for 10 minutes and carve.

Oyster Sauce for a Turkey

"Take a Pint of Oysters, squeeze out the Liquid, which you set aside. Put them in cold water, wash and clean them well and put them in a Terrine with their Liquid. In which you add a kernel of Nutmeg with a little butter, folded into flour, and a quarter of a Lemon; then let them boil".

Aubergines à la Ampère

3 aubergines (eggplants) ~ 3 tablespoons Gruyère cheese (coarsely grated)
2 garlic cloves ~ 6 tablespoons olive oil ~ 6 anchovy fillets
4 oz black olives ~ 1 teaspoon black pepper ~ 3 teaspoons salt

Cut the aubergines in half lengthways and scoop out the flesh of each half. Brush the aubergine shells with olive oil and sprinkle with 2 teaspoons of salt. Arrange them on an ovenproof dish and bake them in a preheated oven at 400°F (gas mark 6) for 15 minutes. Chop up the inside flesh, place it in another ovenproof dish, cover, and bake with the shells for the same time.

Stone the black olives and chop them finely, leaving a few for decoration. Crush the garlic cloves and fry them gently in olive oil. Add the anchovy fillets and mush them into a purée. Add the chopped black olives and the cooked aubergine flesh to the oil, and crush everything into a pulp. Season with black pepper and salt.

Fill the shells with the mixture and sprinkle the Gruyère cheese on top. Cut the remaining black olives in half and decorate the stuffed aubergine shells. Reheat in a 400°F (gas mark 6) oven until the cheese is melted and slightly brown.

Bananes flambées

3 large bananas ~ 2 tablespoons butter ~ 1 teaspoon cinnamon ~ 1 cup rum

Peel the bananas and cut them in half lengthways and dust them with cinnamon. Melt the butter in a skillet and fry the bananas gently, until they are brown on both sides. Drain the butter and heat the rum. Arrange the bananas on a serving plate and pour the rum over them. Light immediately and serve.

[BREAD]

Hunters and gatherers were known in ancient time to eat wild grains, such as barley, wheat, corn or rice. In Neolithic times between 12,000 BC and 10,000 BC people started planting their own crops in settlements, it was then that nomadic peoples became sedentary farming communities. The grains were ground with stones and cooked in water to make a gruel, which was later dried in the sun. These were flat breads, the earliest form of bread, which are still consumed today as *tortillas*, buckwheat or *matzos*. They all were low in gluten, which is needed to make breads rise. The first raised breads must have come haphazardly into existence when a fermented beverage was accidentally added to a flatbread dough, which after resting began to rise.

Ancient Egyptians mastered the craft of baking. Archaeological findings have unearthed grinding stones and bakeries. Tombs along the Nile show images of the planting and harvesting of wheat, which was the most popular grain in Egypt. Various ingredients were added to the bread, such as seeds and spices, also honey, dates and eggs. Later the Greeks, Romans and Saxons became acquainted with bread baking. In the Roman days around the time of Christ, there were some 300 bakeries in Rome, producing a half a million loaves of bread a day. The Romans were the first to perfect the art of grinding with rotary mills, and often flavoured their breads with the seeds of poppy, fennel or cumin. From Rome bread spread throughout the Roman Empire. Later in the Middle Ages the bread-baking trade began to develop with many varieties of loaf. However, it was not until the 17th century when the Dutchman Anthony van Leeuwenhoek, who developed over 247 microscopes, gave the first descriptions of bacteria, protozoa, spermatozoa, and also yeast. This was when the art of bread making turned into a science. During the American colonial period in the 1770s, wheat was the largest export. In 1776 apparently, George Washington's farm at Mount Vernon yielded a wheat crop of over 75 tons. It was not until 1859 when Louis Pasteur, known for his studies on fermentation and bacteria, discovered the exact working of yeast. When the yeast comes into contact with the starch in the flour, it produces carbon dioxide, which in its turn causes the gluten in the flour to expand, and hence the dough to rise.

THE PENNSYLVANIA GAZETTE, October 19, 1752

As frequent Mention is made in the News papers from Europe, of the Success of the Philadelphia Experiment for drawing the Electric Fire from the Clouds by Means of Pointed Rods of Iron erected on high Buildings, &c., it may be agreeable to the Curious to be inform'd, that the same Experiment has succeeded in Philadelphia, tho' made in a different and more easy Manner, which any may try, as follows...

A certain Cure for the Bite of a Mad Dog

Let the Patient be blooded at the Arm nine or ten Ounces. Take of the Herb, called in Latin, "Licken Cinerus Terrestris"; in English, "Ash-coloured Ground Liverwort", cleaned, dried and powdered, Half an Ounce.

Of Black Pepper powdered, two Drachms. Mix these well together, and divide the Powder into four Doses; one of which must be taken every Morning fasting, for four Mornings successively in Half a Pint of Cow's Milk warm. After these four Doses are taken, the Patient must go into the cold Bath or a cold Spring, or River every Morning fasting for a Month. He must be dipt all over, but not stay in (with his Head above Water) longer than Half a Minute, if the Water be very cold. After this he must go in three Times a Week for a Fortnight longer.

N.B. The Licken is a very common Herb, and grows generally in sandy and barren Soils all over England. The right Time to gather it, is in the Months of October and November.

Independence Day Banquet

LETTUCE AND ANCHOVY SOUP

~

STUFFED LIBERTY TURNIPS

~

CHANTERELLES IN MADEIRA

~

DUCK WITH PASSY PURÉE

~

CHICKEN À LA REINE, RED, WHITE AND BLUE

~

YANKEE DOODLE CABBAGE

~

GOOSEBERRY AND FIG COMPOTE

Dr. FRANKLIN, presents his Compliments to
....and desires the honour
of .... Company at Dinner, on Monday the 5th
of *July*; in order to celebrate the ANNIVERSARY of the
DECLARATION of AMERICAN INDEPENDENCE.

Passy, ... 1779

An Answer if you please

Franklin's gala marking the third anniversary of the Declaration of Independence, was attended by many dignitaries, such as Vergennes and the marquis and marquise de Lafayette. Also present were the chevalier de Laneuville and the comte Montfort de Prat, both officers in the American army. Also invited were Franklin's friends and neighbours; the Veillards, the Brillons, the Chaumonts and Barbue-Dubourg. The American contingency consisted of Ralph and Alice Izard, Arthur Lee, Samuel Petrie and Samuel Wharton. The third anniversary, which fell on a Sunday, was celebrated in Passy the following day. Benjamin Franklin had rolled out the red carpet for his guests.

They dined under the watchful eyes of a portrait of George Washington, holding the Declaration of Independence. Benjamin Franklin treated his distinguished guests to an enormous amount of food. There were ducks, three varieties of chicken, including chicken à la reine, turkeys, quails, veal and lamb. Two kinds of pigeons were served with fruits and vegetables. The guests feasted on melons, gooseberries, figs, strawberries and raspberries, apricots, pears and cherries. The vegetables accompanying all this delight were string beans, cucumbers, French peas, lettuce, cabbage, grape leaves, artichokes, carrots, cauliflower, turnips, onions and mushrooms. Bacchus himself was well represented; 136 pints of wine had been purchased to wash down all these fine foods of Independence celebration. The local grocer Gautier delivered butter, sugar, eggs, coffee, anchovies, pickles, mustard, nutmeg, pepper, cloves, vinegar and rice.

There were loyal toasts to the French king and queen in both languages. Songs were sung in honour of the allied forces for their bravery in the defence of liberty, and it was predicted that American Independence Day would be celebrated by many generations to come. Guests were given copies of "La Science du Bonhomme Richard", printed on Franklin's press. After dinner the guests danced to the tunes of a band playing military music.

Lettuce and Anchovy Soup

1 head of Boston lettuce ~ 1 head of Romaine lettuce ~ 4 oz rocket lettuce
2 tablespoons butter ~ 2 teaspoons corn starch ~ 1 pint of vegetable stock
1 pint of chicken stock (see p. 46) ~ 1 oz anchovy strips
2 egg yolks ~ ¼ pint soured cream ~ 1 teaspoon black pepper
1 teaspoon salt ~ 1 teaspoon grated nutmeg

Carefully shred the Boston, Romaine and rocket lettuces. Set half of the rocket lettuce aside for garnishing and chop finely. Take a large enamel saucepan and melt the butter. Add the strips of anchovy and squash them into a pulp. Stir in the nutmeg, pepper and salt, and add some of stock. Blend in the corn starch and add the rest of the vegetable and chicken stock. Add the shredded lettuce leaves and bring to a boil. Simmer for 15 minutes and set aside to cool. Pour the mixture into a food processor and purée. Reheat in the saucepan and blend in the egg yolks and soured cream, without boiling. Pour into a soup terrine and serve with the rest of the shredded rocket leaves garnished on top.

TOAST TO:

"The King of France, illustrious Protector of American Liberty."
"Le Roi de France, illustre Protecteur de la Liberté Americaine."

Stuffed Liberty Turnips

8 young turnips ~ ½ cup diced bacon ~ ½ cup chopped chives
1 tablespoon butter ~ 2 tablespoons lemon juice ~ 1 cup beef stock
½ cup dry sherry ~ ½ cup breadcrumbs
1 teaspoon white pepper ~ 3 teaspoons salt

Hollow out the turnips and cook them in boiling water for 10 minutes. Rinse under cold water, dry with a towel and sprinkle with 2 teaspoons of salt. Fry the diced bacon in butter and purée in a food processor. Fry the diced bacon in butter until crispy and blend in the purée with the chopped chives. Pour in the lemon juice and the dry sherry. Mix thoroughly and season with white pepper and salt. Fill the shells with the purée and arrange them in a well-buttered gratin dish. Pour in the beef stock and coat the turnips with the breadcrumbs.
Place the dish in a 400°F (gas mark 6) oven and cook for 25 minutes.

TOAST TO:

"The Queen, and may they and their Posterity long reign over an affectionate and happy People."
"La Reine puissent ils regner longtems eux et leur Posterité sur un Peuple heureux et affectionné."

Chanterelles in Madeira

8 oz chanterelles ~ 6 shallots ~ 3 cloves of garlic
1 tablespoon chopped fresh parsley ~ 3 thyme sprigs ~ 3 rosemary sprigs
4 tablespoons Madeira ~ 2 tablespoons olive oil ~ 2 tablespoons lemon juice
1 teaspoon white pepper ~ 1 teaspoon salt

Clean the chanterelles with a wet towel and pat dry. Peel and quarter the shallots and slice the garlic cloves. Heat the olive oil in a skillet and gently fry the shallots until just tender. Add the garlic and fry for 2 minutes. Add the chanterelles with the leaves of 2 rosemary and 2 thyme sprigs. Season with the lemon juice, white pepper and salt. Pour in the Madeira, cover and simmer gently till the chanterelles are just cooked. Remove the chanterelles onto a serving dish and sprinkle with chopped parsley. Garnish with the remaining sprigs of rosemary and thyme. Serve with slices of whole-wheat toast.

TOAST TO:

**"The King of Spain and the Rest of the renowned Bourbon Family;
with Success to their Arms".
"Le Roi d'Espagne et toute l'illustre Famille des Bourbons & Succés
à ses Armes."**

Duck with Passy Purée

½ lb strips of roasted duck breast ~ 2 small shallots ~ 1 lb carrots
1 cup red grapes ~ 2 tablespoons butter ~ 1 tablespoon olive oil
2 tablespoons soured cream ~ 2 teaspoons sugar
2 teaspoons chopped parsley ~ 1 teaspoon black pepper
2 teaspoons salt

Slice the carrots and cook them with 2 teaspoons of sugar, 1 teaspoon of salt and 1 teaspoon of butter. When cooked, drain and mash them into a purée. Add black pepper and salt. Just before serving add more butter and soured cream.

Chop the shallots very finely and fry gently in olive oil. Add the strips of duck and reheat them quickly at high temperature.

Spoon the carrot purée onto the middle of a dish and sprinkle with chopped parsley. Arrange the hot strips of duck around the purée. Peel and seed the red grapes and cut them into halves. Decorate the strips of duck with the halves of red grapes.

TOAST TO:

**"The Congress and may they always govern with the same Wisdom
that has hitherto distinguished them."
"Le Congrés. Puisse-t-il toujours gouverner avec la même Sagesse
qui l'a distingué jusqu'a present."**

Chicken à la Reine, Red, White and Blue

1 (4 lb) chicken ~ 1 lb veal forcemeat ~ 3 teaspoons salt
3 teaspoons white pepper ~ 1 teaspoon nutmeg ~ 3 teaspoons butter
6 teaspoons flour ~ 2 pints chicken stock (see p. 46)
1 tablespoon lemon juice ~ ½ pint soured cream ~ ¼ cup diced black truffles
½ cup red currants ~ ½ cup blueberries

Mix forcemeat with 1 tablespoon of butter, 1 teaspoon of white pepper, 1 teaspoon of nutmeg and 1 teaspoon of salt into a homogeneous paste. Stuff the chicken with the forcemeat and cover the skin with lemon juice. Season with white pepper and salt. Arrange the chicken in a shallow casserole and cover with aluminium foil. Preheat oven at 400°F (gas mark 6) and bake for 1 hour.

Melt 2 tablespoons of butter in a saucepan and add the flour. Stir in 1 teaspoon of white pepper and 1 teaspoon of salt. Stir into a thick *roux*. Add the chicken stock bit by bit, constantly stirring with a wooden spoon until a smooth consistency. Blend in the soured cream with the diced black truffles. Simmer until the sauce thickens. Set aside in a double-boiler until needed.

Pour some of the white sauce on a hot serving dish and arrange the chicken on top. Cover the whole chicken with the rest of the sauce and garnish the chicken and the dish, covered in white sauce, with the red currants and blueberries.

TOAST TO:

**"The Marquis de la Fayette and all the brave Strangers who have
hazarded their Lives in our Cause."**
**"Le Marquis de la Fayette et touts les braves Etrangers qui ont
risqué leurs Vies pour notre Cause."**

Yankee Doodle Cabbage

1 Savoy cabbage ~ 1 lb ground veal
1 teaspoon white pepper ~ 1 teaspoon salt ~ ½ teaspoon nutmeg
½ cup cognac ~ 1 large egg ~ 6 strips of streaky bacon
2 cups of chicken stock (see p. 46) ~ 3 cloves

Boil the cabbage for 10 minutes in salt water. Drain and let it cool off. To make the forcemeat, mix the ground veal, egg, white pepper and salt, nutmeg and cognac in a food processor. Purée the mixture until a very smooth consistency. Refrigerate until required.

Peel off the large outer leaves of the cabbage and cut off the hard parts. Chop the leaves of the inner part of the cabbage in a food processor and blend with equal parts of the forcemeat into a mixture.

Roll out the large outer leaves and fill them lengthways with a strip of the mixture. Roll them up into a long flute and secure them with kitchen string on both ends and twice in the middle.

Line a casserole with 3 bacon strips and place the cabbage flutes on top. Pour in the stock and cover with 3 more strips of bacon. Drop in the cloves and bring to a boil. Put the casserole in a preheated oven at 350°F (gas mark 4) and cook for 90 minutes.

TOAST TO:

"Generals Washington, Gates, Arnold and all the valiant Americans who have fought in Defence of their Country."
"Les Generaux Washington, Gates, Arnold et touts les vaillans Americains qui ont combattu pour la Defense de leur Patrie."

Gooseberry and Fig Compote

½ lb gooseberries ~ 2½ cups sugar
4 fresh figs ~ 1 cup orange blossom liqueur
2 tablespoons lemon juice

Place the gooseberries in a saucepan with 1 cup of sugar and 2 cups of water and bring to a boil. Make a syrup by mixing 1½ cups of water with the orange blossom liqueur and 1½ cups of sugar. Place the figs in the syrup and cook for 3 minutes. Drain the gooseberries and arrange them on a serving dish. Place the figs on top. Reduce the syrup and pour over the figs and gooseberries.

TOAST TO:

"The combined Fleets of France & Spain, and may Fame swell their Sails, and Victory crown all their Enterprizes."
"Les Flottes combinées de France et d'Espagne; Puisse la Renommée enfler leurs Voiles et la Victoire couronner toutes leurs Entreprises."

Three positions of the Elbow, an illustration by Franklin's grandson Temple proving that, since God gave men elbows, he intended them to drink.

Here is a *Drinking Song* made for a dinner given to Benjamin Franklin at Madame Helvétius's in Auteuil in 1779 around Independence Day, composed by the Abbott André Morelett:

In history all alone
The name Franklin is etched in stone,
I would like you to sing along
In this glorious drinking song,
Glass in hand to begin:
Let us sing to our Benjamin.

In politics he is great
And dines happily in debate,
An Empire melted down in half
You should see him drink and laugh,
Glass in hand to begin:
Let us sing to our Benjamin.

Like the audacious eagle flies
He has taken to the skies,
Took away the thunder
That threatened the ground under,
Glass in hand to begin:
Let us sing to our Benjamin.

Wild America deserved
Its liberty preserved,
Half of this accomplishment
Is due to our temperament,
Glass in hand to begin:
Let us sing to our Benjamin.

There was never any fight
For a greater right;
They wanted Independence
To drink the wines of France,
Glass in hand to begin:
Let us sing to our Benjamin.

The English without humanity
Wanted to turn them into tea;
They sold them wine of trouble,
And made them pay double,
Glass in hand to begin:
Let us sing to our Benjamin.

Congress has declared
They would drink our claret,

And for the sake of our champagne
They have started their campaign,
Glass in hand to begin:
Let us sing to our Benjamin.

When you see our heroes bravely beat
The English and their fleet,
'Tis to make America fine
Drink our Catholic wine,
Glass in hand to begin:
Let us sing to our Benjamin.

These English, great in their spirits
Are profound in all their writing wits,
They know from where the winds blow
But their cooking is oh so low,
Glass in hand to begin:
Let us sing to our Benjamin.

We often see them, as they can
Try to kill their fellow man,
They become morally bad
For need of wine, they are sad,
Glass in hand to begin:
Let us sing to our Benjamin.

We can throw into the sea
This people's pride, and see,
But with our victory on the brink
We shall teach them how to drink,
Glass in hand to begin:
Let us sing to our Benjamin.

[TRUFFLE]

The truffle was known to the ancient Egyptians, as well as to the Greeks and Romans. It was believed to have medicinal and magical powers and was also used as an aphrodisiac. During the Middle Ages, however, the truffle fell from grace, when it was regarded as being the work of the devil on earth. Later during the Renaissance it regained popularity, especially by Louis XIV. Truffles were then often cooked in wine as an appetiser, and served on a bed of flower petals. Truffles grow mainly on the roots of oak trees and feed off the trees' nutrients. They have to be found and dug up with the help of the olfactory skills of trained pigs or dogs, a practice which dates back to the 17th century. Despite attempts to cultivate truffles, they still have to be found in the wild, the old-fashioned way. This has become increasingly a problem since the beginning of the 20th century owing to continuing deforestation.

Cultivated Garden

GARDEN SALAD

~

GARDENER'S CHICKEN

~

GARDEN COMPOTE

~

JUS DE CAROTTES DU JARDINIER

Voltaire, who had praised Benjamin Franklin as a champion of liberty, was also one of the first to have had a lightning rod installed at his home. Like Franklin, he had also been a frequent diner at Le Procope in the rue de l'Ancienne-Comédie, where he had his own marble-slab table. Voltaire had spent a few turbulent years with Frederick the Great at the Court of Prussia, where one day he received a note in the form of a rebus from Frederick saying:

$$\frac{P}{\text{Venez}} \quad à \quad \frac{Ci}{\text{Sans}} \quad \text{(Venez Souper à Sans Souci)}$$

Voltaire's reply read:

$$J'AI \quad a \qquad \text{(J'ai Grand Appétit)}$$

Benjamin Franklin had commented on Voltaire's *Traité sur la tolérance* (1763) with the words: "There is in it abundance of good Sense and sound Reasoning, mix'd with some of those Pleasantries that mark the Author as strongly as if he had affix'd his Name." When Voltaire had come to Paris on his final visit in 1778 to put on his last tragedy *Irene*, the philosopher received Benjamin Franklin and his grandson Temple at once and gave them his blessing. This happened in spite of warnings to Franklin from Louis XVI, who saw Voltaire's free-thinking, liberal philosophies as a threat to the French nation. Benjamin Franklin and Voltaire both belonged to the same Masonic lodge, les Neuf Sœurs. They met again publicly in late April at the Académie des Sciences. The two men embraced each other to great public applause; how enchanting it was to see Solon and Sophocles embracing!

After Voltaire's death later that year Franklin attended a commemorative Masonic ceremony held by the Lodge of the Nine Sisters in honour of the French author. Franklin attended, again despite the objections of the King and the government. The French clergy even remained opposed to the burial of Voltaire; hence his embalmed body remained in a vault of an abbey in Champagne until 1791 when it was interred in the Pantheon in Paris. The commemoration took place at the lodge's seat in the rue du Pot-de-Fer-Saint-Sulpice and started with the initiation of new members, amongst whom was the painter Jean-Baptiste Greuze whose portrait of Franklin adorns the jacket of this book. By great Masonic exception there were two women in the audience during the ceremony. One was Madame Denis, a niece of Voltaire's with whom he had had a love affair some 40 years before. She presented the lodge with a bust of Voltaire by the sculptor Jean Antoine Houdon, who had also immortalized Franklin with a bust portrait in 1778. The poet Roucher, who later on would fall victim to the Terror, read some clearly anti-clerical passages from his new work and finally a huge painting was unveiled depicting the glorification of Voltaire. The gathering proceeded to move to the next-door banquet room, where Roucher was asked to recite more of his poetry. The "Doctor who tamed Lightning" was directly alluded to in the line: "The captivated Thunder died at its Feet", which aroused a standing ovation. The Masonic Lodge of the Nine Sisters was later to be disciplined by the Grand Orient for allowing women to be exposed to the Masons in their aprons with full regalia. The Nine Sisters were expelled from their seat and all their possessions were thrown out, including the Houdon bust. In the following year, however, and perhaps not entirely co-incidentally, the dispute was settled just one day before Franklin took over as Worshipful Master of the lodge.

The closing words of Voltaire's *Candide* "Il faut cultiver notre jardin" [We must cultivate our garden] perhaps mirror Franklin's own philosophy.

> "Happy the Man whose wish and care
> A few paternal Acres bound
> Content to breathe his native Air
> In his own Ground"

Garden Salad

½ head of lettuce ~ 1 cucumber ~ 2 carrots
2 tablespoons chopped mint leaves
½ cup finely chopped spring onions (scallions) ~ 4 ripe tomatoes
¼ lb French beans

Dressing:

4 tablespoons olive oil ~ 4 tablespoons lemon juice
1 crushed clove of garlic ~ 1 tablespoon Dijon mustard ~ 1 teaspoon salt
2 teaspoons pepper ~ 1 teaspoon sugar ~ 1 teaspoon anchovy essence
4 teaspoons crushed pine kernels

Wash and dry the vegetables. Parboil the beans and set aside to cool. Skin and seed the tomatoes and cut them into thin slices. Cut the carrots into fine strips and slice the cucumber. Arrange broken pieces of lettuce in a shallow salad dish. Put a layer of beans on top, in the middle and surround them with the shredded carrot. After mixing the cucumber and tomato slices, place them over the beans.

For the dressing; mix all the ingredients well together and pour over the salad. Top the salad with the spring onions, followed by the mint leaves.

Gardener's Chicken

4 chicken drumsticks ~ 4 chicken thighs ~ 3 oz bacon strips
2 chopped red onions ~ 8 quartered cloves of garlic ~ ½ cup mushrooms
4 chopped tomatoes, seeded and skinned ~ 4 tablespoons olive oil
2 teaspoons salt ~ 2 teaspoons ground black pepper ~ 2 teaspoons sugar
3 bay leaves ~ 1 teaspoon rosemary ~ 1 teaspoon thyme
10 coarsely chopped fresh basil leaves ~ ½ cup red wine

Skin the drumsticks and thighs. Heat olive oil in a casserole and quickly brown the pieces on all sides for 5–7 minutes. Remove the chicken pieces from the casserole and drain on a towel. Fry the strips of bacon in the oil until crisp, then add the chopped onions and quartered cloves of garlic and sauté until light brown. Add the mushrooms, tomatoes, salt and pepper, sugar, rosemary, thyme and bay leaves. Stir in the red wine and bring back to the heat, while stirring thoroughly. Return the chicken pieces to the mixture, cover the casserole and simmer for 40 minutes, stirring from time to time. Serve on a platter and garnish with coarsely chopped basil leaves.

Garden Compote

In the 1700s berry fruits were mostly made into jams, and used as preserved spreads to go on bread, being much cheaper than butter. Currants were used in puddings and cakes, and garden rhubarb, which came from Italy, was put into tarts. Favourite fruits were gooseberries and damsons.

2 cups strawberries ~ 2 cups gooseberries ~ 2 cups damsons
2 cups black cherries ~ 3 peaches
3 tablespoons icing sugar ~ 2 tablespoons rum ~ 2 tablespoons kirsch

Put the strawberries and gooseberries in a colander, pick over and rinse with cold water. Remove the stones from the damsons and cherries, and rinse with cold water. Peel the peaches and remove the stones. Mix all five fruits in a large glass serving bowl. Sprinkle with sieved icing sugar and refrigerate.

Mix the rum and kirsch together with the fruit salad just before serving.

Jus de carottes du jardinier

1 lb carrots ~ 1 small onion ~ 1 medium turnip ~ 2 cloves garlic
½ cup lemon juice ~ ½ cup lime juice
1 teaspoon zest of lemon ~ 1 teaspoon zest of lime
¼ cup chopped coriander/cilantro

Push the carrots, quartered onion, garlic cloves, coriander and turnip through a juicer. Add the juices and the zests of the lemon and lime. Stir thoroughly and leave to chill in the refrigerator. When it is ice cold, serve in highball glasses.

[VEGETABLES]

In the days of Voltaire and Franklin, many of the vegetables that we know today were available, for example cabbages, turnips, carrots, parsnips and onions. There were artichokes, garden peas, cauliflower and celery. People ate lettuce, watercress, French beans, cucumber and spring onions. Tomatoes were first discovered as a weed in the maize fields in the New World and were not eaten in Europe until the late 18th century and then only when cooked. The first tomatoes that were brought back to Europe were yellow, thence the Italian name *pomodoro* [golden apple]. Later the Jesuits sailed back from the Americas with red tomatoes. In America it was Thomas Jefferson who first started to cultivate tomatoes in his garden at Monticello. By the end of the 19th century people in Europe finally started to eat tomatoes raw as well. Raw fruit was finally acknowledged by the medical world to be a safe and healthy food; hitherto it was believed to cause colic and spread the plague.

THE PENNSYLVANIA GAZETTE. May 9. 1734

Advertisement

Very good single Refin'd Loaf Sugar sold reasonable by the great or small Quantity, at the Printer's hereof. Also Coffee, and Cases of Bottles.

Receipt against the Plague

"Take of Rue, Sage, Mint, Rosemary, Wormwood and Lavender, a Handful of each; infuse them together in a Gallon of White Wine Vinegar, put the Whole into a Stone-pot closely covered up, upon warm Wood Ashes for four Days: After which draw off (or strain through a Flannel) the Liquid, and put it into Bottles well corked; and into every Quart Bottle, put a Quarter of an Ounce of Camphire.

With this Preparation wash your Mouth, and rub your Loins and your Temples every Day; snuff a little up your Nostrils when you go into the Air, and carry about you a Bit of Spunge dipped in the same, in order to smell to upon all Occasions, especially when you are near any Place or Person that is infected. They write, that four Malefactors (who had robbed the infected Houses, and murdered the People during the Course of the Plague) owned, when they came to the Gallows, that they had preserved themselves from the Contagion, by using the above Medicine only; and that they went the whole Time from House to House, without any Fear of the Distemper."

Dutch Treat

BROILED HERRINGS

~

DUTCH BEEF

~

LEYDEN HUTSPOT

~

CHESTNUT PURÉE WITH CARAMELIZED APPLE

~

GENEVER

In the summer of 1761 Benjamin Franklin toured the Austrian Netherlands, visiting Brussels, Ghent and Bruges with his son William and his friend Richard Jackson. They also travelled to the Dutch Republic, passing through Delft, The Hague, Leiden, and Haarlem, before reaching Amsterdam. In The Hague they were received with great civility by the British Ambassador Sir Joseph Yorke and dined in company of Count Willem Bentinck, Chairman of the College of Deputies of the States General. In Leiden they visited Professor Peter van Musschenbroek who had discovered the Leyden Jar: "Mr Musschenbroek's wonderful Bottle" as Dr Franklin called it. William Franklin later wrote to his sister Sarah about the journey:

> "The Most disagreable Circumstance I met with in Holland, was their Continual Smoaking of Tobacco. I don't Recollect that I saw more than one Dutch Man without a Pipe in his Mouth, and that was a fellow who had hung in Chains so long that his Head had drop'd off. There very Children are taught Smoakin from the Moment they leave Sucking, and the Method they take to teach them is, to give them when they are Cutting their Teeth, an Old Tobacco pipe which is smoak'd Black and smooth to rub their Gums with insted of Coral."

On their way back to England on a overcrowded small sloop, they sprang a leak and had to keep the pumps going continuously. The party landed 60 miles further from London than they had expected. However, they made London just in time for the coronation of George III, to which they had been invited.

In 1781 the Dutch government was still pro-British. Stadholder William V was a cousin of George III, but Amsterdam and its merchants were supportive of the American Revolution. They were making good money by trading arms, intelligence and goods to the Patriots through the Dutch Caribbean islands St Eustatius and Curaçao. About this kind of practice Benjamin Franklin concluded:

> "Holland is no longer a Nation, but a great Shop, and I begin to think it has no other Principles or Sentiments but those of a Shopkeeper."

In a letter to Governor Francis Bernard, Benjamin Franklin wrote:

> "… I have no Receipts for Pickling either Sturgeon or Salmon, but will endeavour to procure you one for Sturgeon. In my Opinion a great deal depends on the kind of Salt to be used. For this I would refer you to Brownrigg's Book where you may find what Salt the Dutch use for their Herrings. There is an alcaline corrosive Quality in common coarse Salt, which must be corrected by some Acid, in the Boiling or Refining of it. The Dutch use Buttermilk, I think for that purpose…"

Broiled Herrings

"Scale the Herrings, gut them, and cut off their Heads. Wash them clean, and dry them in a Cloth. Flour the Herrings and broil them, but with your Knife just notch them across: Take the Heads and mash them, and boil them in small Beer or Ale, with a little Whole Pepper and Onion. Let it boil a Quarter of an Hour, then strain it. Thicken it with Butter and Flour and a good deal of Mustard. Lay the Fish in a Dish, and pour the Sauce into a Bason, or use plain melted Butter and Mustard."

"Haring in 't Land, de dokter aan de Kant"
[A Herring a Day, keeps the Doctor away] *not* BENJAMIN FRANKLIN

Dutch Beef

"Take the lean part of a Buttock of Beef raw, rub it well with Brown Sugar all over, and let it lye in a Pan or Tray two or three Hours, turning it two or three Times. Then salt it well with common Salt and Salt-petre, and let it lye for a Fortnight, turning it every Day. Then roll it very strait in a coarse Cloth, put it in a Cheese-press a Day and a Night, and hang it to dry in a Chimney. When you boil it, you must put it in a Cloth; when it is cold, it will cut in Slivers as *Dutch* Beef."

Leyden Hutspot

On 3rd October 1574, during the Spanish siege of Leiden, a young boy went outside the city walls to find out why it had got so quiet on the besieged Spanish ramparts. The Spanish had left hurriedly overnight and there was a pot of stew meat, abandoned by the departing Spanish soldiers. After months of siege, the hungry boy ate the whole pot. That is why, still today, the people of Leiden eat Hutspot on 3rd October. Today potatoes are used in Hutspot, but they were not in the original recipe since potatoes were still unknown in Europe in 1574.

2 lbs stewing beef ~ 2 onions chopped ~ 2 cups white beans
1 cup sliced parsnips ~ 1 cup sliced carrots ~ 1 cup dried prunes
½ cup chopped parsley ~ 4 oz butter
2 teaspoons salt ~ 2 teaspoons pepper
2 teaspoons grated nutmeg ~ 2 teaspoons grated ginger
4 tablespoons lemon juice ~ 4 tablespoons orange juice

Cut stewing beef into 1-inch pieces and simmer in a casserole with butter and a little water (or beef stock) with the onions till cooked. Stir in pepper, salt, ginger and nutmeg. Add prunes (soaked and drained), carrots, white beans (soaked and drained) and the parsnips. Add lemon and orange juices. When necessary add more water and/or stock. Cover casserole and simmer for an hour or until all the vegetables are cooked and the meat is falling apart into little strings. Stir in the parsley and serve.

Chestnut Purée with Caramelized Apple

1 lb chestnuts ~ ½ pint of milk ~ 1½ oz butter ~ 2½ oz sugar
1 apple ~ 9 oz sugar ~ 1 tablespoon lemon juice
9 fl oz heavy cream ~ 2 oz fine sugar ~ 2 egg whites
1 teaspoon of cinnamon

Cross the skins of the chestnuts with a sharp knife and put them in a pan with enough water to cover them. Bring the water to a boil and let it cook gently for 10 minutes. Take them out and peel them and add the milk. Bring it back to a boil and let it simmer for ½ hour. Rub the chestnuts through a sieve and put the purée in a saucepan. Blend in the butter and the 2½ oz of sugar and spread the purée in a circle on a round 9-inch platter to cool off. Peel and core the apple and slice it into 16 equal parts. Melt the 9 oz of sugar with some water and the lemon juice in a stainless steel saucepan, while tilting the pan for even cooking and browning of the sugar.

When the liquid has turned to an even and desired colour, prick a wooden skewer through a piece of the apple, tilt the saucepan and dip it into the liquid caramel. Repeat this until all the slices of apple are covered with caramel, and set them aside. Whip the heavy cream with the 2 oz of fine sugar until stiff and fold in the equally stiff beaten egg whites. Arrange the caramelized pieces of apple evenly around the edge of the chestnut purée and garnish the centre with a huge blob of the freshly and lightly whipped cream and dust it off with the cinnamon.

"A good general Rule in travelling in foreign Countries, is, to avoid as much as possible all Disputes, and to be contented with such Provisions and Cookery as you meet with in the Inns, so you will have the best the Country affords in the Season, which you cannot know so as to direct, and if you attempt to direct the Cookery they will not understand or be able to follow your Orders, and whatever Difficulties you put them to they will be sure to charge you extravagantly for, particularly in Holland."

Benjamin Franklin in a letter to Isaac Smith, May 17, 1771

[SPICES]

In prehistoric times the use of leaves, nuts, fruits and barks was known to enhance the taste of meats. In Mesopotamia we know that spices such as caraway, sesame, fennel, cardamom and saffron were used; their seeds have been found at archaeological sites. The ancient Chinese used spices especially in medicine. Star anise and ginger are among the oldest Chinese spices, and as far back as 300 BC the Chinese were known to obtain nutmeg, mace, cinnamon and cloves from the Moluccan Islands, later known as the Spice Islands. In Roman cookery ginger was a favourite spice, caraway roots were a popular vegetable, and the scarce quantities of pepper were cut with crushed juniper berries. However, it was the Arabs whose trade with the Spice Islands brought spices back to the Middle East, and later during the Crusades medieval Europeans came in contact with the spices of the East, of which cloves, nutmeg and pepper became highly valued as preservatives and flavour enhancers for food and drink. Spices were then also known for their medicinal effects against rheumatism, gout and colic. And oranges studded with cloves were supposed to be a good protection against the plague. By the end of the Middle Ages when the Venetians were controlling the importing of spices into Europe, the demand for oriental spices was rapidly increasing in Europe and the supply was low. When pepper finally reached Venice, its price had increased many times over during its trip. By then the Europeans started to search for sea routes to the Spice Islands to enable them to take charge of the trade. Christopher Columbus went westwards in 1492 and discovered, not India, but the Americas. However, it was Vasco da Gama, who set sail from Belem in 1497 and successfully navigated around Africa and discovered the sea route to India and the Spice Islands. As a result of the new spice trade Lisbon had soon replaced Venice as the mercantile and spice centre of Europe. Later during the second half of the 16th century the Portuguese first lost the Moluccan Islands to the Spanish, who were to be replaced by the Dutch in 1605, who held on to their monopoly for almost 350 years.

[GENEVER]

Genever was invented for medicinal purposes in 1650 by Dr Franciscus de la Boie, a professor at the University of Leiden. Known as Dr Sylvius, he was seeking an inexpensive medicine for the treatment of kidney disorders. He mixed unaged grain alcohol with the oils of the juniper berry and called it genever, after the French word for juniper. During the time when English soldiers were fighting on the Continent, they discovered genever, which gave them "Dutch Courage" in battle. This new drink was brought back to England, where the population grew very fond of the new spirit, which soon acquired the shortened name of "gin".

POOR RICHARD'S ALMANAK

The thrifty maxim of the wary Dutch,
Is to save all the Money they can touch.

৻৶৶ ৻৶৶ ৻৶৶

THE PENNSYLVANIA GAZETTE, August 17. 1738

Advertisement Phila. the 14th of the 6th Mo. 1738

All Bakers of Loaf Bread and Housekeepers in the City of Philadelphia are hereby advertised, that the Weight of Bread is appointed as follows, and so to continue till there shall be further Reason to alter the Weight, viz.

The 5 penny Loaf White Bread, 38 Ounces and three quarters.

The 5 penny Loaf of Wheaten or Midling Bread, 60 Ounces Troy Weight, to which all Bakers are required to confrm themselves.

Receipt for how to preserve Meat in hot Weather, without Salt
By Benjamin Franklin

A Clean Cloth dipp'd in Vinegar, and wrapt close round a Joint of Meat, Dr. Boerhaave says, will keep it good eight Days.

Don Saltero's Salsa

SWIMMING PASTA

~

CHOUDER, A SEA DISH

~

CHELSEA BISCUITS

~

ICED TEA

On the banks of the Thames in Chelsea lived a Mr Salter, servant of Sir
Hans Sloane, physician to the king and prominent member of the Royal
Society of Arts. Mr Salter had established himself as a barber on Cheyne
Walk in 1695. He had taken in all kinds of papers and musical instruments
from Sir Hans and made his place into a small museum. A Vice-Admiral
Munden, just back home from years of service on the Spanish coast had
nicknamed him "Don Saltero", a name he carried with him to the grave.
Don Saltero's museum was not only a barber's shop, but a gathering place,
a coffee house and a reading room. Men of standing came to Don Saltero's
to have a shave or sip a cup of coffee. In 1723, just after Daniel Defoe's book
Robinson Crusoe had become the talk of the town, Don Saltero advertized his
attractions thus:

Monsters of all sorts here are seen
Strange things in Nature as they grew so,
Some relics of the Sheba Queen,
And fragments of the famed Bob Crusoe.

Knick-Knacks, too, dangle round the wall
Some in glass cases, some on shelf,
But what's the rarest sight of all?

YOUR HUMBLE SERVANT SHOWS HIMSELF.

Richard Cromwell, the son of Oliver Cromwell and who contributed his father's sword, used to come and sit in silence for hours. The museum included such rarities as tiger's tusks; a candle of the pope; the skeleton of a guinea-pig; the King of Morocco's tobacco pipe; Queen Elizabeth's prayer book; Mary Queen of Scot's pincushion and a pair of nun's stockings. One day in 1725 the young Benjamin Franklin, who was still working for Palmer's in Bartholomew Close paid a visit to the museum. He had just sold a purse to Sir Hans Sloane, made out of stone asbestos from the loyal colonies, who in turn had added it to his collection. Benjamin in return had received an invitation to visit the museum, and went to Chelsea by water with his young printer friend Wygate to see Don Saltero's collection.

"They introduc'd me to some Gentlemen from the Country who went to Chelsea by Water to see the college and Don Saltero's Curiosities. In our Return, at Request of the Company, whose curiosity Wygate had excited, I stript and leapt into the River, and swam from Chelsea to Blackfryars, performing on the Way many Feasts of Activity both upon and under Water, that surpriz'd and pleas'd those to whom they were Novelties. I had from a Child been ever delighted with this Exercise, had studied and practis'd all Thevenot's Motions and Positions, added some of my own, aiming at the graceful and easy, as well as the Useful. All these I took this Occasion of exhibiting to the Company, and was much flatter'd by their Admiration. And Wygate, who was desirous of becoming a Master, grew more and more attach'd to me, on that account, as well as from the Similarity of our Studies."

Swimming Pasta

1 lb ground veal meat ~ 1 Italian hot sausage
2 cloves of crushed garlic ~ 1 large finely chopped onion
½ cup diced celery ~ 1 cup diced tomatoes ~ ½ cup chopped fennel
½ cup diced green bell peppers ~ ½ cup dry white wine
1 teaspoon oregano ~ 1 bay leaf
1 teaspoon salt ~ 2 teaspoons fresh ground pepper
4 oz tomato paste ~ ½ cup olive oil ~ ½ lb *fettuccini*
1 cup green olives stuffed with anchovy paste

Skin the hot sausage and break it up into pieces. Sauté the veal and sausage in a saucepan, in olive oil with garlic, onion, salt and pepper until brown. Add the celery, tomatoes, bell peppers, fennel and sauté until partially cooked. Add the dry white wine and bay leaf and set to simmer. Stir in the oregano, salt and pepper and tomato paste and keep simmering until all the vegetables are cooked and the sauce thickens.

Boil the *fettuccini* till well cooked, way past the current *al dente* fashion, drain and pour the sauce over the fettuccini. Top with green olives filled with anchovy paste.

Chouder, a Sea Dish

"Take a Belly-piece of pickled Pork, slice off the fatter Parts, and lay them at the Bottom of a Kettle, strew over it Onions, and such sweet Herbs as you can procure. Take a middling large Cod, bone and slice it as for Crimping, Pepper, Salt, All-spice, and Flour it a little, make a Layer with part of the Slices; upon that a slight Layer of Pork again, and on that a Layer of Biscuit, and so on, pursuing the like Rule, until the Kettle is filled to about four Inches. Cover it with a nice Paste, pour in about a Pint of Water, lute (seal) down the Cover of the Kettle, and let the Top be supplied with live wood Embers. Keep it over a slow Fire about four Hours.

When you take it up, lay it in the Dish, pour in a Glass of hot Madeira Wine, and a very little India Pepper. If you have Oysters, or Truffles and Morels, it is still better; thicken it with Butter. Observe, before you put this Sauce in, to skim the Stew, and then lay on the Crust, and send it to Table reverse as in the Kettle; cover it close with the Paste, which should be brown."

BENJAMIN FRANKLIN BOOK OF RECIPES

Chelsea Biscuits

1 lb flour ~ ½ lb powdered sugar
1 lb currants ~ 10 tablespoons heavy cream ~ 3 egg yolks
3 tablespoons dry white wine
1 teaspoon mace powdered fine ~ ½ lb butter

Rub the butter into the flour and mix in the sugar and currants. Then add the cream and egg yolks. Pour in the dry white wine and the mace. Make the mixture into a well worked up paste and set in a dish before a fire or oven, until it is warm through. Make it into little cakes and put them onto a well-buttered baking tray, prick a hole in the top. Bake them quickly in a pre-heated 400°F (gas mark 6) oven until golden brown.

Iced Tea

1 quart water ~ ⅓ cup Ceylon Dimbula tea leaves
2 tablespoons lemon juice ~ 1 tablespoon lime juice
1 tablespoon sugar
2 slices of lemon ~ 4 mint leaves

Put the tea leaves in a heated pot and pour in boiling water. Brew uncovered for 5–7 minutes and add sugar and the lemon and lime juice. Stir and leave to cool at room temperature. Serve over lots of ice, so the tea gets really cold, and garnish with lemon slices and the mint leaves.

> *"Use now and then a little Exercise a quarter of an Hour before Meals, as to swing a Weight, or swing your Arms about with a small weight in each Hand; to leap, or the like, for that stirs the Muscles of the Breast"*
> BENJAMIN FRANKLIN

[TEA]

In Chinese mythology tea came into existence in 2737 BC when a leaf from a tea plant descended into the water one of his servants was boiling while the Emperor Chen Nung was sitting in this garden. The Emperor decided to try the new brew and liked it. Since then tea has become the national drink in China. The tea plant can grow up to 30 feet and at first monkeys were trained to pick the leaves and throw them down. Later the plant was kept up to 3–4 feet high for picking purposes. Today there are more than 1,500 varieties of tea grown in 25 different countries, of

[154]

which India, Sri-Lanka, Kenya, Indonesia and China are the main producers. It was not until the late 16th century that tea reached Europe, when the Portuguese and the Dutch became the first traders. In England the first records show tea dealings with Chinese merchants in 1644. Tea was brought back from the Far East and first made its introduction in London coffee houses in 1657, the first was offered at Thomas Garraway's in Exchange Alley, between Cornhill and Lombard Streets. Tea was then sold as an agent against "gripping of the guts" the common cold. Surveys claimed it could make the human body healthy, active and lusty. Tax was levied on tea by the mid-18th century and had reached a peak of nearly 120%. This was very unpopular among the tea drinking population and resulted in a booming tea smuggling trade, especially from Holland and Scandinavia. Even the smuggled tea was expensive, and in 1777 it could cost up to 10s 6d per pound. In 1784, William Pitt the Younger cut the taxes on tea from 120% to 12.5% and effectively ended the trade in smuggled tea.

Tea drinking was as popular in the American colonies as in Britain. First in 1767 the Townsend Act was passed, imposing taxes on tea, glass, lead, oil and paint, with the aim of raising some £40,000 a year in revenue for the British army. Then in 1773, when Lord North imposed a tax on tea and coffee, further resentment was created amongst the colonists for not having any representation in Parliament, which by law could levy taxes in the colonies. The Tea Act of 1773 also gave the East India Company the right to import tea from China directly to the American colonies for sale directly to retailers, which put many American tea importer out of business. So on 16th December 1773 tea was left to rot on the docks of Charleston and fifty to sixty men disguised as Mohawk Indians boarded the ships of the East India Company, broke open the wooden tea chests and hurled them overboard. The party had just begun.

[PASTA]

Pasta, the mixture of flour and water, finds its origin in China, supposedly brought to Venice by Marco Polo. The Arabs claim to have introduced dried pasta to Sicily. In the 15th century a Chinese priest brought buckwheat into Japan, that later developed into a new type of pasta called *soba*, which is green and thin. In the late 18th century *soba* shops in Japan were designed to look more like the traditional tea houses, making the consumption of soba more respectable. European countries have modelled their pastas on Italian style, while in southeastern Asia Chinese noodles are more popular. Pastas in the form of *vermicelli* and *macaroni* were first introduced in England in the 18th century and came from Italy. Today Italy boasts 600 pasta shapes with their own accompanying sauce. Tubular pastas, like *ziti* and *penne*, come from southern Italy, while their flattened brothers, fettuccini and lasagna, are from northern stock.

THE PENNSYLVANIA GAZETTE, 1745

Advertisement

Choice Bohea Tea to be sold by the Dozen or half Dozen Pound, at the Post-Office, Philadelphia.

Receipt for the Fever and Ague
By Benjamin Franklin

Take two Ounces of Jesuits Bark, one Ounce of Snakeroot, one Ounce of Salt of Tartar, and Half an Ounce of Camomile Flowers; put them into a Half Gallon Bottle, filled with Jamaica Spirit, and set it into a Kettle of Water, over a moderate Fire, and let the Ingredients infuse three Days, the Water being kept rather warmer than Blood warm. Dose for a grown Person Half a Jill, three or four times between the Fits; for a Child of a Year old a Tea Spoonful, mixed with Balm Tea; the Quantity to be increased according to the Age of the Person. The Ingredients, by adding more Spirit to them, make a good preventing Bitter.

Chess Board

Benjamin Franklin to William Straham

Philada. Sept 22. 1751

"My Daughter receiv'd her Books all in good Order, and thanks you for your kind Care in sending them. Enclos'd is a second Bill for £20 Sterling. The first went per Mesnard. There is a little Book on the Game of Chess, by Philip Stamma, printed for J. Brindley, 1745. If to be had, please to send it me; with the Remaining Vols. of Viner as fast as they are publish'd.

We are all well, and join in affectionate Regards to you, Mrs Straham and your Children. I am, Dear Sir, Your obliged humble Servant.

(*The Noble Game of Chess; or a new and easy method to play well in a short time,* London 1745).

From Benjamin Franklin to his wife Deborah

New York, April 29, 1757

"Among my Books on the Shelves, there are two or three little Pieces on the Game of Chess; One in French bound in Leather, 8vo. One in a blue Paper Cover, English; the others in Manuscript; one of them thin in brown Paper Cover, the other in loose Leaves not bound. If you can find them yourself, send them: But do not set anybody else to look for them. You may know the French one, by the Word ECHECS in the Titlepage."

Benjamin Franklin was devoted to the game of chess. He often saw the game as a model for diplomatic efforts and wrote a paper on "The Morals of Chess". When he had left Portsmouth, England, he wrote on 22 March 1775 to his son William on board the *Pennsylvania Packet* bound for Philadelphia:

"The new Parliament was to meet the 29th of November. About the Beginning of that Month, being at the Royal Society, Mr Raper one of our Members told me there was a certain Lady who had a Desire of Playing with me at Chess, fancying she could beat me, and had requested him to bring me to her: it was, he said, a Lady with whose Acquaintance he was sure I should be pleas'd, a Sister of Lord Howe's, and he hop'd I would not refuse the Challenge. I said I had been long out of Practice, but would wait upon the Lady when he and she should think fit. He told me where the House was, and would have me call soon and without farther Introduction, which I undertook to do; but thinking it a little awkward, I postpon'd it; and on the 30th meeting him again at the Feast of the Society Election, being the Day after the Parliament met, he put me in Mind of my Promise, and that I had not kept it, and would have me name a Day when he said he would call for me to conduct me. I nam'd the Friday following. He call'd accordingly. I went with him, play'd a few Games with the Lady, whom I found of very sensible Conversation and pleasing Behaviour, which induc'd me to agree most readily to an Appointment for another Meeting a few Days after, tho' I had not the least Apprehension that any political Business could have any Connection with this new Acquaintance.

The Time thus appointed was the Evening of the Day on which I was to have my second Chess Party with the agreable Mrs Howe, whom I met accordingly. After Playing as long as we lik'd, we fell into a little Chat, partly on a Mathematical Problem, and partly about the new Parliament then just met, when she said:

'And what is to be done with this Dispute between Britain and the Colonies? I hope we are not to have a Civil War.'

'They should kiss and be Friends', says I, 'what can they do better? Quarrelling can be of Service to neither but is Ruin to both.'

'I have often said', says she, 'that I wish'd Government would employ you to settle the Dispute for 'em. I am sure no body could do it so well. Don't you think that the thing is practicable?'

'Undoubtedly, Madam, if the Parties are dispos'd to Reconciliation; for the two Countries have really no clashing Interest to differ about. 'Tis rather a Matter of Punctilio, which Two or three reasonable People might settle in half an Hour. I thank you for the good Opinion you are pleas'd to express to me; but the Ministers will never think of employing me in that good Work; they choose rather to abuse me.'

'Ay', says she, 'they have behav'd shameful to you. And indeed some of them are now asham'd of it themselves.' "

From Caroline Howe to Benjamin Franklin

Grafton Street Saturday January 7, 1775

"Mrs Howe's compliments to Dr Franklin, he may depend upon her care. She has just received a letter from Lord Howe, which she wishes to communicate to the Doctor. Business obliges her to be out this morning till one, if it would not be inconvenient to him to call upon her after that hour any time before four, or in the afternoon betwixt 6 and 8 she shall be happy to see him; and she is likewise in hopes of his company at Chess to morrow."

Franklin's Grouse Gambit

1 grouse ~ ½ cup chopped chanterelle mushrooms
1 cup carrots, roughly chopped ~ 2 shallots, roughly chopped
1½ pints of grouse stock ~ 1 cup red wine ~ ¼ pint soured cream
2 tablespoons flour ~ 1 tablespoon chopped parsley
1 teaspoon paprika powder ~ 1 teaspoon salt ~ 1 teaspoon pepper

Take a carving knife and cut the breast off the grouse, along the breastbone on both sides. Remove the skin and set aside. Bring water to a boil and slide the grouse, shallots and carrots into the water. Bring back to a boil, add salt, and simmer covered for two hours, while skimming from time to time the scum from the surface.

Take the bird out and scrape off the leftover eatable pieces of meat. Pour the liquid through a strainer into another pan. Discard the vegetables. Add the pieces of cooked meat. Bring back to a simmer, add salt and pepper, paprika powder. Melt butter in a skillet and fry gently the pieces of breast on both sides until just cooked, then take them out and cut them up into approximately ½ inch pieces. Melt some more butter and add the flour to make a *roux*. Gradually add some grouse stock while still stirring until you have a nice creamy consistency. Add more stock, red wine and the soup. Cut the chanterelles into strips and add them to the pot and cook for 5 minutes. Thicken the soup with soured cream and at the last moment add the cooked pieces of breast. Serve hot and dust off with the chopped parsley.

Mme Petronille Le Roy paid Benjamin Franklin an unexpected visit in Passy. However, Dr Franklin was too preoccupied with his game of chess with M. Le Roy, so he led her to the door. The rain was pouring down and Franklin lent her his umbrella. Mme Le Roy wrote the following letter to Benjamin Franklin in response to his rudeness:

"It was in really poor taste, Mon Cher Papa, to play such a dirty trick last night and to keep Mr. Le Roy and show me the door so cruelly. I shall not expose myself again to having such fun poked at me—something you would not have done to all the society ladies you frequent, particularly when the weather was so bad. I am sure you know all too well how eager I always am to please you and if you had quite simply told me that you wanted to play another game I'd have fallen in with your wishes, even though it was 11 PM and already late for women of delicate health to dine as it can upset their health. But as they aren't selfish, they know how to acquiesce to everything which can be agreeable to society at the risk of their health and their own pleasure. As I don't often have the pleasure of seeing Mr. Le Roy, it is only natural that I wanted to dine with him. It is the only time he gives to me and it happens all too rarely for me not to be upset when I'm deprived of this pleasure. I am returning your umbrella and thank you for it."

Knight's Prawn Salad

1 dozen medium-sized uncooked shrimps ~ 4 tablespoons olive oil
1 tablespoon garlic sauce ~ 1 tablespoon baking soda
2 teaspoons salt ~ 2 teaspoons white pepper powder
$\frac{1}{4}$ cup lemon juice ~ lettuce leaves

Peel the shrimps and take the heads off. Make an incision along the belly and take out the intestine. Rub the shrimps with baking powder and set aside for 10 minutes. Rinse the shrimps thoroughly and pat dry with a towel. Preheat a skillet for 2 to 3 minutes. Pour in the olive oil and wait till it starts to smoke. Stir-fry the shrimps until they change colour. Add the garlic sauce and stir for another 30 seconds. Arrange the lettuce leaves onto a serving dish and place the stir-fried shrimps neatly on top. The shrimps should be eaten by first dunking them into the lemon juice, before dipping them into the salt and pepper dishes.

From Katherine French to Benjamin Franklin

Monday 17th June 1771

"Mrs French understands that Docr Franklin dines with the Bishop of St Asaph's to morrow hopes he will do her the favor of dining with her on Wednesday or Thursday, both days will be giving her a double pleasure, she has provided chess players for each day."

Bishop's *Foie Gras*

½ lb goose (or duck) *foie gras* ~ ½ cup *cornichons*
12 slices whole wheat toast ~ 2 oz butter ~ lettuce leaves

Pâté de foie gras came into existence in the 1780s. In France during the reign of Louis XVI it became fashionable to chop, grind or purée meat and vegetables until they no longer resembled the original product.

Cut the slices of toast in the shape of a mitre. Slice the *foie gras* into 6 half-inch pieces with a hot knife and sandwich each of them between two pieces of mitre-shaped toast. Trim the excess *foie gras*. Butter both outsides of each toast mitre lavishly and take a knife and cut the *cornichons* lengthways into thin strings and studs. Place them in the butter of each mitre to form the cross on the front sides and with stud decorations along the outsides of each side. Arrange the lettuce leaves over 6 plates and place all 6 mitres in the middle of each plate. Serve with a chilled glass of champagne.

From Anne-Louise Brillon de Jouy to Benjamin Franklin

"Madame Brillon would like to have the honour of seeing Monsieur Franklin and to offer him and Monsieur his small son dinner on Thursday.

Comédie Française after dinner in a 'loge grillée' [a private box in which one cannot be seen from the outside] and a game of chess and tea later in the evening."

Queen Anne's Florentine Pie

1 leg of veal ~ 1 teaspoon marjoram ~ 1 teaspoon thyme ~ 1 teaspoon savory
1 teaspoon parsley ~ 1 teaspoon grated nutmeg ~ 1 teaspoon salt
1 teaspoon pepper ~ 1 medium onion, finely chopped
2 cloves of garlic, crushed ~ 1 manchet, grated (small roll of white bread)
4 egg yolks ~ 4 slices of streaky beacon ~ 3 bay leaves
1 tablespoon oyster sauce ~ 1 deep piecrust, with lid ~ 1 beaten egg

Take a leg of veal and cut it into thin slices. Season the slices with sweet marjoram, thyme, savory, parsley, rosemary, nutmeg, chopped onion and crushed garlic. Mix the manchet crumbs, salt and pepper and the egg yolks into a consistent paste. Spread this mixture well over the slices of veal and lay them into a piecrust, intermixed with layers of streaky bacon. Put in the bay leaves and sprinkle the oyster sauce over it. Close the crust with the lid, prick a few holes in it, and glaze with the beaten egg. Chill while preheating the oven to 450°F (gas mark 8). Bake for 30 minutes, then cover the pie loosely with some aluminium foil to prevent blackening. Turn heat down to 325°F (gas mark 3) and bake for another 30 minutes until the pie is cooked.

From Benjamin Franklin to Anne-Louise Brillon de Jouy

Saturday November 29, 1777, 11 o'clock at night

"Having got back home I was surprised to find out it was almost 11 o'clock. I am afraid we forgot all other things because of too much attention to our game of chess. We have inconvenienced you too much by holding you up too long in the bath. Tell me, my dear friend, how are you this morning? Never shall I consent to start a game hereafter in your bathroom. Would you forgive me for this indiscretion?"

King George's Pudding

1 pint of milk ~ strip of lemon peel ~ 3 cloves ~ 1½ oz long grain rice
1 oz caster sugar ~ 2½–3 lbs stewed apples ~ 5 fl oz white wine
1 oz butter ~ 1 oz candied lemon and orange peel ~ 5 eggs, separated
2 baked puff pastry cases, each 8 inches wide

Bring the milk to a boil, with the lemon peel and cloves. Add the rice and simmer over gentle heat until tender, after about 40 minutes. Remove the cloves and lemon peel, sweeten with the sugar and add the stewed apples, wine, butter, candied peel and lastly the egg yolks. Whisk the egg whites till stiff and fold into the mixture. Spoon into the baked puff pastry shells. Bake in a 350°F (gas mark 4) oven for 35–40 minutes, or until golden brown and the filling is set. Serve with a wine sauce.

"Never spare the Parson's wine, nor the Baker's Pudding"
BENJAMIN FRANKLIN

Benjamin Franklin to William Straham

Philada. June 20. 1752

"… Honest David Martin, Rector of our Academy, my principal Antagonist at Chess, is dead, and the few remaining Players here are very indifferent, so that I have now no need of Stamma's 12s Pamphlet, and am glad you did not send it."

Morals of Chess (June 1779)

The game of Chess is not merely an idle amusement. Several very valuable qualities of the mind, useful in the course of human life, are to be acquired or strengthened by it, so as to become habits, ready on all occasions. For life is a kind of chess, in which we have often points to gain, and competitors or adversaries to contend with, and in which there is a vast variety of good and ill events, that are, in some degree, the effects of prudence or the want of it. By playing at chess, then we may learn:

1. *Foresight*, which looks a little into futurity, and considers the consequences that may attend an action; for it is continually occurring to the player, "If I move this piece, what will be the advantages or disadvantages of my new situation? What use can my adversary make of it to annoy me? What other moves can I make to support it, and to defend myself from his attacks?"

2. *Circumspection*, which surveys the whole chess-board, or scene of action, the relations of several pieces and situations, the dangers they are respectively exposed to, the several possibilities of their aiding each other; the probabilities that the adversary may make this or that move, and attack this or the other piece; and what different means can be used to avoid his stroke, or turn its consequences against him.

3. *Caution*, not to make our moves too hastily. This habit is best acquired, by observing strictly the laws of the game; such as, *if you touch a piece, you must move it somewhere; if you set it down, you must let it stand.* And it is therefore best that these rules should be observed, as the game thereby becomes more the image of human Life, and particularly of war; in which, if you have incautiously put yourself into a bad and dangerous position, you cannot obtain your enemy's leave to withdraw your troops, and place them more securely, but you must abide all the consequences of your rashness.

And *lastly*, we learn by chess the habit of *not being discouraged* by *present* appearances in the state of our affairs; the habit of *hoping for a favourable change*, and that of *persevering in the search of resources.* The game is so full of events, there is such a variety of turns in it, the fortune of it is so subject to sudden vicissitudes, and one so frequently, after long contemplation, discovers the means of extricating one's self from a supposed insurmountable difficulty, that one is encouraged to continue the contest to the last, in hopes of victory by our own skill; or at least, of giving a *stale mate*, by the negligence of our adversary. And whoever considers, what in chess he often sees instances of, that particular pieces of success are apt to produce *presumption*, and its consequent, inattention, by which more is afterwards lost than was gained by the preceding advantage, while misfortunes produce more care and attention, by which the loss may be recovered, will learn not to be too much discouraged by the present success of his adversary, nor to despair of final good fortune, upon every little check he receives in the pursuit of it.

That we may, therefore, be induced more frequently to chuse this beneficial amusement, in preference to others which are not attended with the same advantages, every circumstance, that may increase the pleasure of it, should be regarded; and every action or word that is unfair, disrespectful, or that in any way may give uneasiness, should be avoided, as contrary to the immediate intention of both the players, which is, to pass the time agreeably.

Musical Glasses

SAUTÉED GLASS EELS

~

RABBIT STEW ADAGIO

~

SAUCE FOR RABBIT JOINTS

~

LEONORA'S STRUDEL

Benjamin Franklin had an interest in music which he had inherited from his father, who played the harp, guitar and violin. He liked simple music and in Craven Street recovering from an illness, he started to experiment with what he called 'Glassy-Chord' or 'Armonica'. Musical Glasses were not unknown in Europe at the time. In the 1740s the Irishman Richard Puckeridge had given concerts by hitting glasses with sticks and rubbing them with his wet fingers. Puckeridge was still performing at the time when Benjamin Franklin arrived in England in 1757. Franklin's fellow Royal Society member Edward Delaval had brought Musical Glasses to his attention. As a scientist and inventor Benjamin Franklin set out to design a playable instrument and by 1762 his Glassy-Chord was brought into production. Thomas Penn, son of William Penn and powerful Proprietary placeman of Pennsylvania, was all too happy to report that his adversary Benjamin Franklin was spending all his time on "philosophical matters and on musical performances on glasses." When Dr Franklin sailed back to Philadelphia he packed up one instrument to take with him. In 1764 a certain Stephen Forrage gave a concert in Philadelphia, introducing the Armonica to Franklin's home town.

During the latter part of the 18th century Musical Glasses were a rage throughout Europe. The German composer Gluck made his famous *Glasspiel* appearance with an earlier form of musical glasses on 23 April 1746 during a concert at the Haymarket Theatre in London. It was advertized as:

> "A Concerto upon Twenty-six Drinking-Glasses, tuned with Spring-Water, accompanied with the whole Band, being a new instrument of his own Invention; upon which he performs whatever may be done on a Violin or Harpsichord, and thereby hopes to satisfy the Curious, as well as Lovers of Musick."

Mozart first played the Glassy-Chord at a garden concert in Vienna at the age of seventeen. His father Leopold was so taken by the sound of the instrument, that he wanted to buy one for the young Wolfgang, but could not afford one. Mozart had first heard the tone of the armonica when the Austrian physician Friedrich-Anton Mesmer played the Musical Glasses. Mesmer was a proponent of a controversial pseudo-medical procedure, which he called "Animal Magnetism". During these seances Mesmer would touch patients with a magic rod at the parts where they were diseased. When a patient, as a result of this procedure, went into a convulsion, it was a sign that "Animal Magnetism" had worked. Essential during these seances was the presence of soft and soothing background music like that of the armonica. Mozart was so delighted by the sound that he composed "Adagio and Rondo for Glass Armonica" and "Adagio for Armonica solo". Ludwig von Beethoven also wrote music for the Armonica to accompany a brief melodrama in the play *Leonora Prohaska* by Friedrich Duncker in 1814. It is said that this melodrama is Beethoven's only work for the Glass Armonica. *Leonora Prohaska*, however, never reached the stage. It is said that it could not pass the censors at the time. With her sister Cecilia, Marianne Davies gave concerts on the armonica throughout Europe, reaching a climax in Vienna when they performed and sang at the wedding of the Archduchess Amalia and the Duke Ferdinand of Parma. The armonica became so popular that even Marie-Antoinette took up the instrument as a student of Marianne Davies. Eventually these Musical glasses went out of vogue and in some German towns the armonica was banned by the police; they were thought with their sweet tones to have a harmful effect on the players and even to cause nervous breakdowns. Benjamin Franklin describes this new instrument to Giambatista Beccaria (1716–1781) professor of physics at Turin.

London, July 13, 1762

> You have doubtless heard the sweet tone that is drawn from a drinking glass, by passing a wet finger round its brim. One Mr Puckeridge, a gentleman from Ireland, was the first who thought of playing tunes, formed these tones. He collected a number of glasses of different sizes, fixed them near each other on a

table, and tuned them by putting into them water, more or less, as each note required. The tones were brought out by passing his fingers round their brims. He was unfortunately burnt here, with his instrument, in a fire which consumed the house he lived in. Mr E. Delaval, a most ingenious member of our Royal Society, made one imitation of it, with a better choice and form of glasses, which was the first I saw or heard. Being charmed with the sweetness of its tones, and the music he produced from it, I wished only to see the glasses disposed in a more convenient form, and brought together in a narrower compass, so as to admit a greater number of tones, and all within reach of hand to a person sitting before the instrument, which I accomplished, after various intermediate trials, and less commodious forms, both of glasses and construction, in the following manner.

The glasses are blown as near as possible in the form of hemispheres, having each an open neck or socket in the middle. The thickness of the glass near the brim about a tenth of an inch, or hardly quite so much, but thicker as it comes nearer the neck, which in the largest glasses is about an inch deep, and an inch and half wide, these dimensions lessening as the glasses themselves diminish in size, except that the neck of the smallest ought not to be shorter than half an inch. The largest glass is nine inches diameter, and the smallest three inches. Between these are twenty-three different sizes, differing from each other a quarter of an inch in diameter. To make a single instrument there should be at least six glasses blown of each size; and out of this number one may probably pick 37 glasses, (which are sufficient for 3 octaves with all the semi-tones) that will be each either the note one wants or a little sharper than the note, and all fitting so well into each other as to taper pretty regularly from the largest to the smallest. It is true there are not 37 sizes, but it often happens that two of the same size differ a note or half in tone, by reason of a difference in thickness, and these may be placed one in the other without sensibly hurting the regularity of the taper form.

The glasses being chosen and every one marked with a diamond the note you intend it for, they are to be tuned by diminishing the thickness of those that are too sharp. This is done by grinding them round from the neck towards the brim, the breadth of one or two inches as may be required; often trying the glass by a well tuned harpsichord, comparing the tone drawn from the glass by your finger, with the note you want, as sounded by that string of the harpsichord. When you come near the matter, be careful to wipe the glass clean and dry before each trial, because the tone is something flatter when the glass is wet, than it will thereby tune to great exactness. The more care is necessary in this, because if you go below your required tone, there is no sharpening it again but by grinding somewhat off the brim, which will afterwards require polishing, and thus increase the trouble.

The glasses being thus tuned, you are to be provided with a case for them, and a spindle on which they are to be fixed. My case is about three feet long, eleven inches every way wide within at the biggest end, and five inches at the smallest end; for it tapers all the way, to adapt it better to the conical figure of the set of glasses. The case opens in the middle of its height, and the upper part turns up by hinges fixed behind. The spindle which is of hard iron, lies horizontally from end to end of the box within, exactly in the middle, and is made to turn on brass gudgeons at each end. It is round, an inch in diameter at the thickest end, and tapering to a quarter of an inch at the smallest. A square shank comes from its thickest end through the box, on which shank a wheel is fixed by a screw. This wheel serves as a fly to make the motion equable, when the spindle, with the glasses, is turned by the foot like a spinning wheel. My wheel is of mahogany, 18 inches diameter, and pretty thick, so as to conceal near its circumference about 25 lb. of lead. An ivory pin is fixed in the face of this wheel and about 4 inches from the axis. Over the neck of this pin is put the loop of the string that comes up from the moveable step to give it motion. The case stands on a neat frame with four legs.

To fix the glasses on the spindle, a cork is to be fitted in each neck pretty tight, and projecting a little without the neck, that the neck of one may not touch the inside of another when put together, for that would make a jarring. These corks are to be perforated with holes of different diameters, so as to suit that part of the spindle on which they are to be fixed. Then a glass is put on, by holding it stiffly between both hands, while another turns the spindle, it may be gradually be brought to its place. But care must be taken that the hole be not too small, lest in forcing it up the neck should split; nor too large, lest the glass not being firmly fixed, should turn or move on the spindle, so as to touch and jar against its neighbouring glass. The glasses thus are placed one in another, the largest on the biggest end of the spindle which is to the left hand; the neck of this glass is towards the wheel, and the next goes into it in the same position, only about an inch of its brim appearing beyond the brim of the first; thus proceeding, every glass when fixed shows about an inch of its brim, (or three quarters of an inch, or half an inch, as they grow smaller) beyond the brim of the glass that contains it; and it is from these exposed parts of each glass that the tone is drawn, by laying a finger upon one of them as the spindle and glasses turn round.

My largest glass is G a little below the reach of a common voice, and my highest G, including three compleat octaves. To distinguish the glasses the more readily to the eye, I have painted the apparent parts of the glasses within side, every semitone white, and the other notes of the octave with the seven prismatic colours, viz C, red; D, orange; E, yellow; F, green; G, blue; A, Indigo; B, purple; and C, red again; so that glasses of the same colour (the white excepted) are always octaves to each other.

This instrument is played upon, by sitting before the middle of the set of glasses as before the keys of a harpsichord, turning them with the foot, and wetting them now and then with a spunge and clean water. The fingers should first be a little soaked in water and quite free from all greasiness; a little fine chalk upon them is sometimes useful, to make them catch the glass and bring out the tones more readily. Both hands are used, by which means different parts are played together. Observe, that the tones are best drawn out, when the glasses turn from the ends of the fingers, not when they turn to them.

The advantages of this instrument are, that the tones are incomparably sweet beyond those of any other; that they may be swelled and softened at pleasure by stronger or weaker pressures of the finger, and continued to any length; and that the instrument, being once well tuned, never again wants tuning.

In honour of your musical language, I have borrowed from it the name of this instrument, calling it the Armonica.

Benjamin Franklin

Sautéed Glass Eels

¼ lb glass eels, per person ~ 4 tablespoons olive oil
3 cloves garlic, crushed ~ 1 teaspoon salt

Glass eels belong to the *Anguillidae* family, they are fresh water eels that undertake a long migration to spawn in the sea. Where the rivers meet the sea is where the eels are caught. They are considered a delicacy especially in Spain.

Heat a skillet with olive oil and sauté the crushed garlic. When the garlic is light brown, stir in the glass eels and cook them a few minutes until they are just done. Sprinkle over some salt and serve at once on some lettuce leaves, with a small wooden fork, which will prevent the eels from slipping through on their way from plate to mouth.

Rabbit Stew Adagio

2 lbs rabbit joints on the bone ~ 3 shallots, chopped ~ 2 cloves garlic, crushed
2 large carrots, peeled and finely diced ~ 2 large potatoes, peeled and diced
2 beef tomatoes ~ 1 cup small mushrooms ~ ¼ lb bacon, diced
1 lb Brussels sprouts ~ 1 tablespoon flour ~ 2 oz butter
1 bundle of sweet herbs ~ ½ pint vegetable stock ~ 2 cups port
2 teaspoon salt ~ 2 teaspoons ground black pepper ~ 1 teaspoon allspice
1 teaspoon fresh chopped parsley

Sprinkle some salt and pepper over the rabbit joints and coat them with flour. Melt the butter in an enamel saucepan and brown the joints on all sides. Add the chopped shallots, garlic, bacon, mushrooms, diced carrots and potatoes, salt, pepper and allspice and fry for 4 minutes. Pour in the vegetable stock and port. Add the bundle of sweet herbs and bring to a boil. Reduce the heat, cover, and simmer very slowly (adagio) for 2½ hours, until the rabbit is tender and easily comes off the bone. Take the joints and the bundle of sweet herbs out of the saucepan and scrape the meat from the bones. Skin and seed the beef tomatoes and cut them into roughly one-inch pieces. Put the meat pieces back in the pan and add the Brussels sprouts and tomatoes. Simmer uncovered for another ½ hour, until the stew thickens. Serve the stew garnished with the chopped fresh parsley.

Sauce for Rabbit Joints

"When your Rabbit Joints are browned, you should pour boiled Onions over them, which you prepare the following way. Take some Onions, peel and fry them. Bring a large Pot of water to a boil, and add the fried Onions to the water and let them boil for about two Hours. Take them out and place them in a Strainer to drain. Then it's time to cut them up on a Table and put them in a Saucepan, dust them with some Flour, add a little bit of Milk or Creme, with a good chunk of Butter , and place it on a flame, and stir until the Butter is melted. Then you pour it all over your Rabbit Joints".

Leonora's Strudel

6 oz flour ~ 1 lb apricots, peeled and stoned ~ 1 cup raisins
4 tablespoons apricot jam ~ 1 teaspoon cinnamon ~ ½ teaspoon salt
½ teaspoon nutmeg ~ ½ teaspoon cloves ~ 2 tablespoons olive oil
3 tablespoons butter ~ 4 oz sugar ~ 1 egg, beaten

Put the flour and salt in a large glass bowl, with the beaten egg and the oil in the middle. Adding some water, knead this into a dough. When the dough no longer sticks to the sides of the bowl, take it out and lay it on a floured surface. Knead the dough for another 10 minutes. Roll the dough into a ball and cover with a cloth and leave it to rest for an hour in a warm place.

Mix the apricots with the raisins in a bowl. Add the apricot jam, sugar and the ground cinnamon, nutmeg and cloves. Mix this thoroughly.

Place a clean kitchen towel on a surface and sprinkle with some flour. Roll the dough out over the towel, in a rectangular shape and about ⅛ inch thick. Melt the butter and brush it over the rolled-out dough. Spread the apricot mixture out over the dough and fold in the edges. Lift up the towel and roll up the strudel, while patting it into shape. Shape the strudel into a crescent and lay it on a greased baking tray. Brush it with some more melted butter and bake in a pre-heated 375°F (gas mark 5) oven for about 45 minutes until brown. Sprinkle the strudel with powdered sugar and serve hot with cold cream.

Turin 20. May 1771

> "I thank *you*, most excellent Sir, for the exact description of *your* new and really harmonious harpsichord with glasses, which *you* have sent me (to *you* it is given to enlighten human minds with the true principles of the electric science, to reassure them by *your* conductors against the terrors of thunder, and so sweeten their senses with a most touching and suave music); and if I were entitled to it I would thank you in the name of Italy, for having given the appellation of Armonica to your agreeable instrument, in consideration of our harmonious language."

> Giambatista Beccaria

BRISTOL JOURNAL, 1762

Advertisement

> "The celebrated *Glassy-Chord* invented by Mr Franklin, of Philadelphia; who has greatly improved the Musical Glasses, and formed them into a compleat Instrument to accompany the Voice; capable of a thorough Bass, and never out of Tune. Miss Davis, from London, was to perform in the Month of January, several favourite Airs, English, Scotch and Italian, on the *Glassy-Chord* (being the only one of the Kind that has yet been produced) accompanied occasionally with the Voice and German Flute."

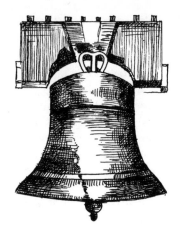

E Pluribus Unum

LIFE-SUSTAINING DIAMONDBACK TERRAPIN SOUP

~

LIBERTY BELL PEPPERS

~

THE PURSUIT OF CHOCOLATE HAPPINESS

~

ORANGE SHRUB

It is said that the "miraculous" document, created by the Founding Fathers of America — the Declaration of Independence, the Constitution and the Bill of Rights — was left vague on purpose, so future generations could interpret it to their own changing circumstances. Perhaps: although Benjamin Franklin demonstrated to the Constitutional Convention in Philadelphia on September 17, 1787, that we all are convinced we are right in our own opinions. However, to form a consensus and to make manifest the delegates' unanimity, signatures could only be put under a document that reflected the common denomination of those delegates at the time. Hence, specific in broad terms, while omitting details.

Here is how Dr. Franklin, "in Order to form a more perfect Union, establish Justice, insure domestic Tranquillity, provide for the common Defence, promote the general Welfare, and secure the Blessings of Liberty to ourselves and our Posterity", eloquently put human fallibility into discourse:

"Mr President,

I confess, that I do not entirely approve of this Constitution; but, Sir, I am not sure I shall never approve it; for, having liv'd long, I have experienc'd many Instances of being obliged, by better Information or fuller Consideration, to

[171]

change my Opinions even on important Subjects, which I once thought right, but found to be otherwise. It is therefore that, the older I grow, the more apt I am to doubt my own Judgement of others. Most Men, indeed, as well as most Sects in Religion, think themselves in Possession of the Truth, and that wherever others differ from them, it is so far error. Steele, a Protestant, in a dedication, tells the Pope, that the only Difference between our two Churches in their Opinions of the Certainty of their Doctrine, is, the Roman Church is infallible, and the Church of England is never in the wrong. But, though many private Persons think almost as highly of their own Infallibility as that of their Sect, few express it so naturally as a certain French Lady, who, in a little Dispute with her Sister, said, 'But I meet with nobody but myself that is always in the Right.' '*Je ne trouve que moi qui aie toujours raison.*'

"In these Sentiments, Sir, I agree to this Constitution, with all its Faults – if they are such; because I think a general Government necessary for us, and there is no *Form* of Government but what may be a Blessing to the People, if well administered; and I believe, farther, that this is likely to be well administered for a Course of Years, and can only end in Despotism, as other Forms have done before it, when the People shall become so corrupt'd as to need despotic Government, being incapable of any other. I doubt, too, whether any other Convention we can obtain, may be able to make a better Constitution; for, when you assemble a Number of Men, to have the Advantage of their own Wisdom, you inevitably assemble with those Men all their Prejudices, their Passions, their Errors of Opinion, their local Interest, and their selfish Views. From such an Assembly can a *perfect* Production be expect'd? It therefore astonishes me, Sir, to find this System approaching so near to Perfection as it does; and I think it will astonish our Enemies, who are confound'd like those of the Builders of Babel and that our States are on the Point of Separation, only to meet hereafter for the Purpose of cutting one another's Throats. Thus I consent, Sir, to this Constitution, because I expect no better, and because I am not sure that it is not the best. The Opinions I have had of its *Errors* I sacrifice to the public Good. I have never whisper'd a Syllable of them abroad. Within these Walls they were born, and here they shall die. If every one of us, in returning to our Constituents, were to report the Objections he has had to it, and Endeavour to gain Partisans in support of them, we might prevent its Being generally receiv'd, and thereby lose all the salutary Effects and great Advantages resulting naturally in our Favour among foreign Nations, as well as among ourselves, from our real or apparent unanimity. Much of the Strength and Efficiency of any Government, in procuring and securing Happiness to the People, depends on *Opinion*, on the general Opinion of the Goodness of that Government, as well as of the Wisdom and Integrity of its Governors. I hope, therefore, for our own Sakes, as a Part of the People, and for the Sake of our Posterity, that we shall act heartily and unanimously in recommending this Constitution, wherever our Influence may extend, and turn our future Thoughts and Endeavours to the Means of having it *well administer'd.*

On the whole, Sir, I cannot help expressing a Wish, that every Member of the Convention who may still have Objections to it, would with me on this Occasion doubt a little of his own Infallibility, and, to make *manifest* our *unanimity*, put his Name to this Instrument."

Life-Sustaining Diamondback Terrapin Soup

2 diamondback terrapins ~ 1 teaspoon chopped parsley
1 teaspoon salt ~ 1 teaspoon pepper ~ ½ teaspoon grated nutmeg
½ tablespoon flour ~ 2 tablespoons butter ~ 1 teaspoon celery salt
1 sherry shaker

Take two diamondback terrapins, about 12 inches long. Cut off the heads right behind the skull. Put them in a pot of boiling water for 7 minutes. Remove and cut off the belly shell. Skin out the legs, tail and neck meat and remove the developed eggs (if you got a female). Put the meat and eggs in a quart of boiling water. Add the parsley, salt and pepper and boil for 20 minutes. Take out the meat and cut into fine pieces. Take one cup of the stock and put it in the refrigerator. Take a frying pan and melt the butter, add the flour and make a *roux*, while stirring well. Take ½ cup of stock from the refrigerator and add bit by bit to the *roux*, until smooth. Add the second ½ cup, until a creamy consistency. Add the terrapin pieces with the eggs and the stock, while still stirring. Season with nutmeg and celery salt. Serve with the sherry shaker.

Liberty Bell Peppers

1 red, 1 green, 1 yellow, 1 orange bell (sweet) pepper
2 cloves garlic, crushed ~ 2 shallots, finely chopped ~ ½ lb ground veal
1 beef tomato, chopped ~ ½ cup mushrooms, chopped
2 oz pine kernels ~ 4 tablespoons virgin olive oil
4 oz Vermont cheddar cheese, grated
2 oz breadcrumbs ~ 1 teaspoon salt ~ 1 teaspoon pepper
1 tablespoon parsley, freshly chopped ~ 1 teaspoon Tabasco

Cut the tops off of the bell peppers and take out the cores and seeds. Discard the tops and wash the peppers and pat them dry with a towel. Heat the olive oil in a skillet and sauté the garlic and shallots until they start to change colour over medium heat. Stir in the ground veal and sauté until brown. Add the chopped beef tomato and mushrooms, with salt and pepper and add the Tabasco. Stir for 2 minutes over medium heat and set aside to cool. Blend in the pine kernels, breadcrumbs, grated cheddar and parsley and form a thick mixture. Brush a shallow baking dish with olive oil. Stuff the bell peppers with the mixture and stand them up in the baking dish. Bake in a pre-heated 375°F (gas mark 5) oven for 35–40 minutes.

The Pursuit of Chocolate Happiness

¼ cup butter ~ 12 oz chocolate, unsweetened ~ ¾ cup sugar
¼ cup flour ~ ½ teaspoon cinnamon ~ 3 eggs ~ 1 tablespoon dark rum
1 cup chopped pecans and walnuts

Melt the chocolate in a double boiler and add the cinnamon and dark rum. Set aside. Cream the butter with the sugar, beat in the eggs and add the melted chocolate. Sieve the flour and stir it into the mixture. Stir in the chopped walnuts and pecans and pour the whole mixture into a pie shell. Bake in a pre-heated 375°F (gas mark 5) oven for about 30 minutes. Serve with whipped cream.

Orange Shrub

By Benjamin Franklin

"To a Gallon of Rum two Quarts of Orange Juice and two pound of Sugar – dissolve the Sugar in the Juice before you mix it with the Rum – put all together in a Cask shake it well – let it stand 3 or 4 Weeks it will be very fine fit for Bottling – when you have Bouled off the fine pass the thick thro a Philtring Paper put into a Tunnell – that not a drop may be lost.

To obtain the flavour of the Orange Peel paire a few Oranges put it in Rum for 12 hours – put that Rum into a Cask with the others.

For Punch thought better without the Peel."

In the 18th century oranges contained not as many sweet juices as the ones we find today in the markets. Therefore, I propose the two pound of sugar, which Franklin suggests we add to a gallon of rum and two quarts of orange juice, should be omitted in order to create a right balance; just what the Doctor ordered. On August 22nd 1999 Chester Kerr passed away, the editor emeritus of Yale University Press. Chester played a key part in publishing the first 21 volumes of The Papers of Benjamin Franklin and it was through his kindness that Mary Bessborough was presented with those issues as a gift for a future library at the Benjamin Franklin House in Craven

Street. It was especially at Chester Kerr's insistence that every milestone of a Benjamin Franklin project ought to be celebrated with a toast of orange shrub. Therefore, I suggest that everyone, after reading this book, break out the orange shrub made from Franklin's own recipe and have a joyful celebration, just like Chester would have done: he always kept a barrel of it in his garage.

[CHOCOLATE]

Chocolate, or "The Food of the Gods", finds its origins as early as 600 AD in the jungles of the Yucatan and Central America. The fruit of the evergreen tree *Theobruma cacao* played an important role in ceremonial rituals, such as marriages, funerals and coming-of-age rites. The cocoa bean was to the Maya and later to the Aztecs what salt had been to the Romans; it was used as currency. Goods were paid for in cocoa beans.

Christopher Columbus was the first European to discover chocolate, during his fourth voyage to America in 1502, when he landed on the coast of Nicaragua. However, he chose to ignore this very bitter drink and it was not until 1519 when Hernán Cortés had a taste of "xocoatl" when he was received by the last Aztec emperor Montezuma. After imprisoning Montezuma and claiming his country for the Spanish crown, Cortés and his conquistadors returned to Spain in 1528, introducing the cocoa bean to the Spanish Court. When Pope Pius V was served a cup of chocolate in 1569, he found it so disgusting that he proclaimed it to be permissible to drink during Lent. Soon chocolate began to spread from Spain to other European countries. It became highly popular in the coffee houses of Florence and Venice.

Chocolate was first introduced to the French Court in 1615, when Louis XIII married the Habsburg-Spanish princess Anne of Austria. Before her son Louis XIV married Infanta Maria Theresa, daughter of Philip IV of Spain, he was given a small casket of chocolate by his bride-to-be as an engagement gift. The French fell in love with the new chocolate drink and later Madame de Pompadour, mistress of Louis XV, found that drinking this royal chocolate would warm her temperament and stir her sensuality. As a native Viennese, Marie Antoinette had her private chocolatier sent over from Vienna to prepare her all kinds of chocolate delicacies.

In 1657 the first chocolate shop opened in London in Bishopsgate and the famous London coffee houses also started to serve chocolate. Sir Hans Sloane, the Royal Physician, discovered that chocolate drink would taste considerably better when mixed with milk, instead of water. Sir Hans kept this a secret, but later sold his recipe to an apothecary in London, which later would become a part of Cadbury. John Cadbury introduced the breakfast beverage "Cocoa Nibs", at his tea and coffee shop in Birmingham in 1824. It became so successful that he started to produce it himself and was later joined by his brother Benjamin. In the New World chocolate was first manufactured in the Massachusetts Bay Colony in 1765.

John Hanau and James Baker opened a processing house there. In Holland in 1828, Coenraad van Houten invented the cocoa press, a process that could extract two thirds of the cocoa butter, leaving a dry powder. Before this invention cocoa was a drink with many additives, to counterbalance the fat contents. All sorts of things were added, like potato starch, flour, or corn meal. Even powdered shells or dried moss, and iron rust were added as colour enhancement.

Later in 1847 Joseph Fry & Sons produced the first eating chocolate, although it was rather grainy with a harsh flavour. The Swiss too had made their entrée in the making of chocolate and Daniel Peter produced the first form of milk chocolate in 1875. Not very successfully, because the water in the milk he had added caused the chocolate to disintegrate. Later Henri Nestlé, the maker of evaporated milk, perfected the method. And it was Rudoph Lindt who in 1880 discovered that by adding more cocoa butter to the chocolate it would become smoother in texture, a process called "conching". In 1908 Theodore Tobler created the famous chocolate bar Toblerone.

Milton Hershey started the Hershey Chocolate Company in 1894. He was later called the Henry Ford of the chocolate. Hershey also produced a quality product at an affordable price. When the Great War broke out in 1914, it was the US Army that commissioned American chocolate manufacturers to make 40 lb blocks of chocolate, to be shipped to the army bases. There the blocks were chopped into smaller pieces and distributed among the soldiers on their way to the front.

In Italy the Buitone family had founded the Perugina Chocolate factory in 1907. It is said that Giovanni Buitone had a love affair with an older woman in the 1930s and sent her little love notes hidden in handmade chocolates. These inspired the legendary *Baci* or Kisses that we still enjoy today.

૯ಖ૨ ஈ૪ಖ ૯ಖ૨

PENNSYLVANIA GAZETTE, 1735

Advertisement

To be sold, By the Printer hereof, very good Chocolate at 4s. per Pound by the Dozen, and 4s. 6d. by the single Pound.

૯ಖ૨ ஈ૪ಖ ૯ಖ૨

THE PENNSYLVANIA GAZETTE

VINDEX PATRIAE, a writer in your paper, comforts himself, and the India Company, with the fancy, that the Americans, should they resolve to drink no more tea, can by no means keep that resolution, their Indian corn not affording "an agreeable, or easy digestible breakfast." Pray let me, an American, inform the gentleman, who seems quite ignorant of the matter, that Indian corn, take it for *all in all*, is one of the most agreeable and wholesome grains in the world; that its green ears roasted are a delicacy beyond expression; that *samp* (coarsely broken Indian corn, boiled and eaten with milk and sugar), *hominy* (grains from Indian corn, with the hulls removed broken into meal and boiled), *succotash* (corn kernels and beans cooked together), and *nolehock* (cooked corn meal), made of it, are so many pleasing varieties; and that a *johny* or *hoecake* (cakes made from corn meal), hot from the fire, is better than a Yorkshire muffin. But if Indian corn were as *disagreeable* and *indigestible* as the Stamp Act, does he imagine we can get nothing else for breakfast? Did he never hear that we have oatmeal in plenty, for water gruel or burgoo (thick gruel or porridge); as good wheat, rye, and barley as the world affords, to make frumenty (hulled wheat boiled in milk, with sugar, raisins); or toast and ale; that there is every where plenty of milk, butter, and cheese; that rice is one of our staple commodities; that for tea, we have sage and bawn in our gardens, the young leaves of the sweet white hickery or walnut, and, above all, the buds of our pine, infinitely preferable to any tea from the Indies; while the islands yield us plenty of coffee and chocolate? Let the gentleman do us the honour of a visit in America, and I will engage to breakfast him every day in the month with a fresh variety, without offering him either tea or Indian corn. As to the Americans using no more of the former, I am not sure they will take such a resolution; but if they do, I fancy they will not lightly break it. I question whether the army proposed to be sent among them, would oblige them to swallow a drop more of tea than they chuse to swallow; for, as the proverb says, though one man may *lead* a horse to the water, ten can't *make him drink.* Their resolutions have hitherto been pretty steadily kept. They resolved to wear no more mourning; and it is now totally out of fashion with nearly two millions of people (earlier funerals in Philadelphia customary marks of mourning were omitted); and yet nobody sighs for Norwich crapes, or any other of the expensive, flimsey, rotten, black stuffs and cloths you used to send us for that purpose, with the frippery gauses, loves, ribbands, gloves, &c. thereunto belonging. They resolved last spring to eat no more lamb; and not a joint of lamb has since been seen on any of their tables, throughout a country of 1500 miles extent, but the sweet little creatures are all alive to this day, with the prettiest fleeces on their backs imaginable. Mr VINDEX'S very civil letter will, I dare say, be printed in all our provincial news papers, from Nova Scotia to Georgia; and together will the other *kind, polite,* and *humane* epistles of your correspondents PACIFICUS, TOM HINT, &c. &c. contribute not a little to strengthen us in every resolution that may be of advantage, to our country at least, if not *yours.* HOMESPUN

❧ ❧ ❧

THOMAS JEFFERSON: *Why do you think a Second Chamber is necessary?*

BENJAMIN FRANKLIN: *Why do you tip your Coffee from the Cup to the Saucer?*

THOMAS JEFFERSON: *To cool it.*

BENJAMIN FRANKLIN: *That's why we pour Legislation into The Senate.*

The Master's Voice

DAUPHINY SOUP

~

RICE

~

INDIAN CORN

~

MILK PUNCH

Benjamin Franklin had been a key player in establishing Philadelphia's first fire brigade, the Pennsylvania Hospital, the Academy of Philadelphia which later became the University of Pennsylvania, and the colony's first militia. In 1747 alarming news had reached Philadelphia of activities by French and Spanish privateers along the Delaware River. Benjamin Franklin tried to persuade the Pennsylvania Assembly of the importance of a defence militia by writing the pamphlet "Plain Truth". The Assembly failed to act. Pennsylvania had to be defended against possible attacks by the French or the Spanish during the War of the Spanish Succession, so Benjamin Franklin organized a lottery, with proceeds going to the building of a fort along the Delaware River for the defence of Philadelphia. Having been mainly responsible for the creation of Pennsylvania's newly created militia, and understanding that an army marches on its stomach, Benjamin Franklin created recipes for soup, corn and rice, to be made directly available to the recruited men of the forces.

Dauphiny Soup

By Benjamin Franklin

"A RECEIPT for making *Dauphiny Soup*, which in Turkey is called *Touble*, and with which a great Number of Persons may be Plentifully fed at a very small Expence.

Take a Pound (16 Oz) of Wheat-meal, and knead it with Water a little salted. When the Paste is made, and kneaded so as to be a little soft, divide it in several pieces, about the Bigness of an Egg each: Then spread them out with a Rolling-pin, so as to make the Paste very thin, and place the whole regularly upon a Table.

Have ready upon the Fire a Sauce-pan, or a little Pot, or an Earthen Pipkin, with one Gallon of Water. When the Water grows hot, put in some Salt, and a Quarter of a Pound of Butter or Suet; and when it begins to boil fiercely, throw in your Paste, having first cut in very small Bits; for the more thin and small they are, the more they will swell. And take Care to throw them into that Part of the Water where it boils the most fiercely.

After this a small Fire will be sufficient for making this Soup boil softly for an Hour and a Quarter, or for an Hour and a Half; but it will be necessary to stir it with a Spoon from Time to Time to the very Bottom, in order to prevent its sticking to the Sauce-pan.

If you find it grows too thick, put in some Water, and if it appears to be too thin, sprinkle into it a little Meal. This Soup is agreeable to the Taste, very filling and nourishing; and the Quantity above-mentioned will be sufficient for six Persons, one Half for Dinner, and the rest for Supper. But as what remains after Dinner will become thick and cold, it must for Supper be diluted with a little warm Water, and made warm again upon a small Fire; and Care must be taken not to let it stand long in the Sauce-pan or Pot, lest it should acquire a brassy or iron Taste.

Ten Pounds of Meal made into Paste, will produce 13 Pounds and a Quarter, which prepared as before-mentioned, will be abundantly sufficient for feeding 60 Persons for the whole Day. And for these ten Pounds of Meal, making 13 Pounds of Paste, there must be ten Gallons of Water, two Pounds and a Half of Butter or Suet, and three Quarters of a Pound of Salt.

The better the Wheat-meal is, without, however, being too fine, the more it will swell or increase. But Flour will produce less Paste, and will dissolve too easily in boiling; and if the Meal be too coarse, it will not be tough enough, consequently will not spread thin enough, therefore that Sort of Meal should be chosen, which is commonly made use of for household Bread."

Rice

By Benjamin Franklin

"A RECEIPT for preparing *Rice*, so as therewith to subsist a great Number of Persons at a small Expence.

Rice is known to be one of the best Sorts of Food we have. Some whole Provinces, and even Kingdoms are nourished by it; and in others the People draw more of their Substance from it, than either from Wheat or Rye.

There are several Ways of preparing it for Food, as with Water, with the Fat of the Meat, or with Milk; but whatever Way you may chuse, you must begin with washing and cleaning it well three different Times in warm Water.

In order to prepare, with Water alone, a sufficient Quantity of it for feeding 30 Persons for a whole Day, put five Pounds of Rice in a Sauce-pan, or Pot, with five Gallons of Water, and a proportional Quantity of Salt: Make it boil upon a small Fire for three Hours, stirring it from Time to Time to prevent its sticking to the Vessel, and as you find it thickens pour in by Degrees more warm Water, to the Amount of five Gallons more. These five Pounds will produce sixty Portions or Shares, neither too thick nor too thin, two of which will be sufficient Food for thirty.

In order to prepare with Meat, or the Fat of Meat, a sufficient Quantity of Rice for feeding 30 Persons for a whole Day, put forty Ounces of Meat into the first five Gallons of Water, and after you have made it boil and froth up, throw in your five Pounds of Rice, with the proper Quantity of Salt, after which proceed as before directed; or instead of Meat you may put 20 Ounces of Suet, and the Rice will be equally good.

And in order to prepare with Milk a sufficient Quantity of Rice for feeding 30 Persons for a whole Day, you are to proceed as with Water alone, only leave out a Gallon and a Half of the Water, and make it up with the same Quantity of Milk, first boiled and flected separately by itself, and not to be put in until the last Quarter of an Hour of Boiling.

It is to be understood, that according to the Number of Persons you intend to feed, you are to augment or diminish in Proportion the Dose of Rice, Water, Meat, Suet, or Milk. And the Rice prepared with Water or Suet may be kept for two or three Days; but that with Milk is apt to turn sour the next Day."

Indian Corn

By Benjamin Franklin

"The Natives in America, who in their Huntings, or in the long Marches they sometimes make to meet and fight their Enemies, have nothing to subsist on but a little Meal made of Indian Corn; and that after having subsisted for many Weeks or Months solely on this Diet, they are not only healthful and vigorous, but the Wounds they receive in Battle are cured with surprizing Facility.

To which we may add, That the *Meal made of Indian Corn*, mentioned as the Subsistence of Indian Warriors in their long Marches, is really made of *parched Corn*, pounded fine; and having thus previously passed the Fire, is ready for Food at any Time, when mixed with cold Water, so that no Fire is necessary to dress their Victuals, which if they were to kindle, their Marches or Ambuscades might be discovered by the Smoke or Smell of Burning.

Their Manner of parching the Corn is easy and expeditious. They fill a large Pot or Kettle nearly full of hot Ashes, and pouring in a Quantity of Corn, stir it up with the Ashes, which presently parches and bursts the Grain without much burning. Then the whole is thrown on a coarse kind of wooden Riddle, which separates the parched Grain from the Ashes. Sand heated in a Pot over a Fire will do as well, or better, and is easily separated from the Grain; and the Operation may be repeated till a sufficient Quantity is obtained, on any Occasion.

That six Ounces of Meal should sustain a Man a Day, is not unlikely, when it is considered, that it is almost all capable of being converted into Nourishment; that Nature does not absolutely require *so much* neat Addition daily to the Substance of the Body, and therefore Full-feeders, by frequent Evacuations, discharge great Part of their common Food not completely digested; but where so small a Quantity is admitted, the Discharges will be less frequent, and the Food moving slower through the Intestines, and being retained longer within them, is almost wholly assimilated."

Milk Punch

By Benjamin Franklin

"Take 6 Quarts of Brandy, and the Rinds of 44 Lemons pared very thin; Steep the Rinds in the Brandy 24 Hours; then strain it off. Put to it 4 Quarts of Water, 4 large Nutmegs grated, 2 Quarts of Lemon Juice, 2 Pound of

[181]

double refined Sugar. When the Sugar is dissolv'd, boil 3 Quarts of Milk and put to the rest hot as you take it off the Fire, and stir it about. Let it stand two Hours; then run it thro' a Jelly-bag till it is clear; then bottle it off."

[RICE]

Throughout history, rice has been one of man's most important staples. The origins of rice cultivation are probably native to the Yangtze, Ganges, Tigris and Euphrates deltas. There is archaeological evidence that rice has been feeding man for more than 5,000 years. The first documented account of authorized rice planting by a Chinese emperor dates back around 2800 BC. The rice plant is an annual that needs warmth and abundant moisture and can grow from 2 to 6 feet tall. Today it is estimated that half the world population subsists wholly or partially on rice consumption.

In Benjamin Franklin's lifetime, rice reached the North American colonies by accident. A ship sailing from Madagascar encountered heavy storms and sought refuge in Charleston harbour, South Carolina. As a thank-you token, the captain made a gift of a small amount of "Golde Seed Rice" to a local planter. The rich and flat soil of the Carolinas and Georgia made it ideal for rice plantations. By 1726 "Carolina Golde" became the standard of high-quality rice and the port of Charleston was already exporting around 4,500 tons of "Carolina Golde" rice.

[CORN]

Corn or maize was cultivated by North American Indians as long as 700 years ago and was introduced to European explorers in the 16th century. Corn was the main staple for the Indians and was eaten at every meal. There were different varieties of corn: white, yellow, blue and red. Some of the corn was dried and made into hominy; dried corn soaked in water and parched in hot ashes. Then coarsely ground or broken. Corn meal was used to make cornbread, corn syrup and corn pudding. Or mixed with beans to make succotash. A sweet dish could be made out of boiled corn meal mixed with maple syrup. All parts of the corn were used; the husks were braided and woven to make masks, moccasins, mats and baskets.

[BRANDY]

Whether the ancient Chinese or Egyptians were the first to master the art of turning fruit mash into higher alcohol, is not entirely clear. One thing we know for sure is that the Moors were the first in Europe to establish distillation, during their occupation of southern Spain from 711, until Ferdinand and Isabella took Granada in 1492. The Spaniards, who were already masters in wine cultivation, started to distil in the pot stills left behind by the Moors. In the 16th and early 17th century it was discovered in the Cognac region of France, that distilling sharp and acidic white wines, and after passing it twice through the stills, gave a smooth drinkable brandy especially after storing it in oak casks for a few years. Today more brandy is produced in Spain than any other European country and by far most of it comes from Andalucia in the South. The name "brandy", however, derived from the Dutch word *brandewijn*, meaning "burnt wine".

THE PENNSYLVANIA GAZETTE, May 22, 1755

Advertisement

FORTY-ONE WAGGONS are immediately wanted, to carry each a Load of Oats and Indian-Corn from Philadelphia to Wills's Creek, for which they are to be paid at their Return TWELVE POUNDS each Wagon. Protections and Passes will be given the Waggoners by Authority of the General, to prevent their being impressed, or detained after Delivery of their Loads. They are to set out together on Thursday the 29th Instant. Apply to BENJAMIN FRANKLIN, in Philadelphia.

Note, Several Neighbours may conveniently join in fitting out a Waggon, as was lately done in the Back Counties. If the Waggons cannot thus be obtained, there must be an Impress.

Receipt for how to stop Blood if a Man is wounded in the Woods
By Benjamin Franklin

Powder made of the rotten Heart of a Black Oak, apply'd, will do it immediately. Some Indians carry a little Bag of this Powder when they go to War.

There is also a Kind of Fungus, somewhat like a Horse's Foot, that grows on old Oaks which have been lopped; it should be gathered in August or September, and kept dry. The Way of preparing it, is, to take off with a Knife the white and hard Part, till you find a Substance so soft, as to yield under the Finger like shammy Leather. This is to be divided into Pieces of different Sizes and Thickness: Beat them with a Hammer, to give them a still greater Degree of Softness, so that they may be easily torn with the Finger.

If even a Limb be cut off, one of these Pieces will stanch the Blood, being only applied and pressed against the bleeding Arteries.

Some say, that this Fungus, or Agaric, as 'tis called, is best when it has a greyish Colour on the Outside; tho' the white is very good.

Baskerville *versus* Caslon

The text in this book of recipes has been set in the typeface Baskerville, a typeface designed by the English printer John Baskerville who later became printer for Cambridge University in 1758. John Baskerville and William Caslon were considered the two greatest English type designers of the 18th century. Until John Baskerville decided to devote his love of type forms to the pursuit of the creation of a new font, the art of type design had remained unchanged since Johann Gutenberg had invented movable type in the middle of the 15th century. Baskerville began his professional career teaching writing as a parish schoolteacher and later became a headstone engraver. It was, however, the craft of japanning household metal goods that made him his fortune. Baskerville set out to redesign his printing press and improve the quality of paper making in order to ensure the best possible reproduction of his new typeface. It took him two years to complete his designs and another six to oversee the cutting of his matrices. After proofs were made, he realized that conventional presses could not reproduce the subtleties of his thin strokes and serifs. To make things worse, in the 18th century, paper was made using crude mesh moulds that left lines on the finished paper. This was not suitable for Baskerville's new delicate typeface, so he decided to set up a paper mill on his own land in Birmingham. Here he invented a paper with a smooth surface, made using a fine woven web of wires, which we now know as wove paper. This paper, together with his own invented quick-drying inks, gave the new Baskerville typeface a perfect impression.

Baskerville's typeface was thicker in the heavy strokes, finer in the light ones and sharper at the angles than the more conventional Caslon face. Many conservatives declared it too difficult to read and it took Baskerville many years to win popularity. When he published his Cambridge Bible in 1763, after losing a considerable amount of money on his heart-driven passion, Baskerville included an extract of this letter from Benjamin Franklin whom he had met in Birmingham.

Craven Street, London

Dear Sir,

Let me give you a pleasant Instance of the Prejudice some have entertained against your Work. Soon after I returned, discoursing with a gentleman concerning the Artists of Birmingham, he said you would be a Means of blinding all the Readers in the Nation, for the Strokes of your Letters being too thin and narrow, hurt the Eye, and he could never read a Line of them without Pain. I thought, said I, you were going to complain of the Gloss on the Paper, some object to: No, no, says he, I have heard that mentioned, but it is not that; 'tis in the Form and Cut of the Letters themselves; they have not that natural and easy Proportion between the Height and Thickness of the Stroke, which makes the common Printing so much more comfortable to the Eye. You see this Gentleman was a Connoisseur. In vain I endeavoured to support your Character against the Charge; he knew what he felt, he could see the Reason of it, and several other Gentlemen among his Friends had made the same Observation, &c. Yesterday he called to visit me, when, mischievously bent to try his Judgement, I stept into my Closet, tore off the Top of Mr. Caslon's Specimen, and produced it to him as yours brought with me from Birmingham, saying, I had been examining it since he spoke to me, and could not for my Life perceive the Disproportion he mentioned, desiring him to point it out to me. He readily undertook it, and went over the several Founts, showing me every-where what he thought Instances of that Disproportion; and declared, that he could not then read the Specimen without feeling very strongly the Pain he had mentioned to me. I spared him that Time the Confusion of being told, that these were the Types he had been reading all his Life with so much Ease to his Eyes; the Types his adored Newton is printed with, on which he has pored not a little; nay, the very Types his own Book is printed with, for he is himself an Author; and yet never discovered this painful Disproportion in them, till he thought they were yours.

BENJAMIN FRANKLIN

THE PENNSYLVANIA GAZETTE, Dec. 8, 1737

Advertisement

A HONORARY Reward is proposed to any *Cabalist*, who shall demonstrate that the Letter Z contains more occult virtues than the Letter X.

Benjamin Franklin died in Philadelphia in
1790 at the age of eighty-four.
After a long, exciting and extraordinary life
as a scientist, diplomat, postmaster, politician,
Minister Plenipotentiary from the United
States of America to the Court of France,
and President of the State of Pennsylvania,
he still considered himself a printer and
a man of letters. He also believed in the
resurrection of the body.
This was reflected in his epitaph:

The body of Benjamin Franklin, printer
(Like the cover of an old book
Its contents worn out,
And strip't of its lettering and gilding)
Lies here, food for worms!
Yet the work itself shall not be lost,
For it will, as he believed, appear once more
In a new
And more beautiful edition
Corrected and amended
By its Author!

"Bad Commentators spoil the best of Books,
So God sends Meat (they say) the Devil Cooks"

BENJAMIN FRANKLIN

Select Bibliography

Aldridge, Alfred Owen. *Franklin and his French Contemporaries*. New York: New York University Press, 1957.

Aresty, Esther B. *The Delectable Past: The Joys of the Table, from Rome to the Renaissance, from Queen Elizabeth 1 to Mrs Beeton, menus, manners & recipes of the Past*. London: George Allen & Unwin Ltd., 1965.

Bowen, Catherine Drinker. *The Most Dangerous Man in America: Scenes from the Life of Benjamin Franklin*. Boston: Atlantic Monthly Press/Little Brown & Company, 1974.

Brears, Peter et al. *A Taste of History, 10,000 Years of Food in Britain*. London: British Museum Press in association with English Heritage, 1993.

Dashwood, Sir Francis. *The Dashwoods of West Wycombe*. London: Aurum Press, 1990.

Doonan, Nancy Locke. *Benjamin Franklin's London Milieu*. London, Philadelphia: Nancy Locke Doonan, 1983.

Dubois, Urbain, and Emile Bernard. *La cuisine classique*, 2 vols. Paris: E. Dentu, Editeur, Palais-Royal, 1886.

Ellis, Aytoun. *The Penny Universities. A History of the Coffee-Houses*. London: Secker & Warburg, 1956.

Franklin, Benjamin. *The Papers of Benjamin Franklin*. Vols. 1–14. Edited by Leonard W. Labaree et al. Vols. 15–26. Edited by William B. Willcox et al. Vol. 27 Edited by Claude A. Lopez et al. Vols. 28–33. Edited by Barbara B. Oberg et al. New Haven, CT: Yale University Press, 1959–1990.

Franklin, Benjamin. *The Private Correspondence of Benjamin Franklin*. London: Published from the Originals by William Temple Franklin, 1817.

Franklin, Benjamin. *Benjamin Franklin, His Life as He Wrote it*. Edited by Esmond Wright. Cambridge, MA: Harvard University Press, 1990.

Franklin, Benjamin. *Benjamin Franklin Autobiography and Other Writings*. Edited by Ormond Seavey. Oxford: Oxford University Press, 1980.

Franklin, Benjamin. *Benjamin Franklin. A Biography in His Own Words*. Edited by Thomas Flemming. New York: Harper & Row, 1972.

Franklin, Benjamin. *The Amazing Benjamin Franklin*. Edited by J. Henry Smythe Jr. New York: Frederick A. Stokes Company, 1929.

Franklin, Benjamin. *The Autobiography of Benjamin Franklin* (Unabridged). Mineola, NY: Dover Publications, 1996.

Garlin, Gustave. *Le cuisinier moderne*, 2 vols. Paris: Garnier Frères, Libraires-Editeurs, 1889.

Glasse, Hannah. *The Art of Cookery, made Plain and Easy*. London: Printed and Sold at Mrs. Ashburn's China Shop, etc., fifth edition 1755, and seventh edition 1760.

Humes, James C. *The Wit & Wisdom of Benjamin Franklin*. New York: Harper Perennial, 1995.

Jennings, Francis. *Benjamin Franklin, Politician*. New York: W. W. Norton & Company, 1996.

Lopez, Claude Anne, and Eugenia W. Herbert. *The Private Franklin, The Man and His Family*. New York: W. W. Norton & Company, 1975.

Lopez, Claude-Anne. *Mon Cher Papa*. New Haven, CT: Yale University Press, 1966.

Middlekauff, Robert. *Benjamin Franklin and His Enemies*. Berkeley, CA: University of California Press, 1996.

Pullar, Philippa. *Consuming Passions*. London: Hamish Hamilton Ltd., 1971.

Schama, Simon. *The Embarrassment of Riches*. Glasgow: Fontana Press, HarperCollins, 1987.

Schama, Simon. *Citizens*. Harmondsworth: Viking, Penguin Group, 1990.

Tannahill, Reay. *Food in History*. London: Eyre Methuen, 1995.

Tourtellot, Arthur Bernon. *Benjamin Franklin, The Shaping of Genius. The Boston Years*. New York: Doubleday & Co., 1977.

Wright, Esmond. *Franklin of Philadelphia*. Cambridge, MA: The Belknap Press of Harvard University Press, 1988.

Index

Orange Skrub:

To a Gallon of Rum two Quarts of Orange Juice and
two pound of Sugar — dissolve the Sugar in the Juice before
you mix it with the Rum — put all together in the Cask
shake it well — let it stand 3. or 4 Weeks & it will
be very fine fit for Bottling — when you have Bottled
off the fine pass the thick thro' a filtering Shilling Paper
at into a Funnell — that not a drop may be lost

To obtain the flavour of the Orange Peel pare a
few Oranges & put it in Rum for 12 hours — &
put the Rum into the Cask with the other —
I think the better without the Peel.